VIETNAM STUDIES

THE DEVELOPMENT AND TRAINING OF THE SOUTH VIETNAMESE ARMY, 1950–1972

by

Brigadier General James Lawton Collins, Jr.

DEPARTMENT OF THE ARMY
Washington, D.C., 1975

Library of Congress Catalog Card Number: 74–34409

First Printing

For sale by the Superintendent of Documents, U.S. Government Printing Office
Washington, D.C. 20402 - Price $2.30 (paper cover)
Stock No. 0820–00532

Foreword

The United States Army has met an unusually complex challenge in Southeast Asia. In conjunction with the other services, the Army has fought in support of a national policy of assisting an emerging nation to develop governmental processes of its own choosing, free of outside coercion. In addition to the usual problems of waging armed conflict, the assignment in Southeat Asia has required superimposing the immensely sophisticated tasks of a modern army upon an underdeveloped environment and adapting them to demands covering a wide spectrum. These involved helping to fulfill the basic needs of an agrarian population, dealing with the frustrations of antiguerrilla operations, and conducting conventional campaigns against well-trained and determined regular units.

It is still necessary for the Army to continue to prepare for other challenges that may lie ahead. While cognizant that history never repeats itself exactly and that no army ever profited from trying to meet a new challenge in terms of the old one, the Army nevertheless stands to benefit immensely from a study of its experience, its shortcomings no less than its achievements.

Aware that some years must elapse before the official histories will provide a detailed and objective analysis of the experience in Southeast Asia, we have sought a forum whereby some of the more salient aspects of that experience can be made available now. At the request of the Chief of Staff, a representative group of senior officers who served in important posts in Vietnam and who still carry a heavy burden of day-to-day responsibilities has prepared a series of monographs. These studies should be of great value in helping the Army develop future operational concepts while at the same time contributing to the historical record and providing the American public with an interim report on the performance of men and officers who have responded, as others have through our history, to exacting and trying demands.

The reader should be reminded that most of the writing was accomplished while the war in Vietnam was at its peak, and the monographs frequently refer to events of the past as if they were taking place in the present.

All monographs in the series are based primarily on official records, with additional material from published and unpublished secondary works, from debriefing reports and interviews with key participants, and from the personal experience of the author. To facilitate security clearance, annotation and detailed bibliography have been omitted from the published version; a fully documented account with bibliography is filed with the U. S. Army Center of Military History.

Brigadier General James Lawton Collins, Jr., presently the Chief of Military History, U.S. Army, has the wealth of experience required to tell the story of allied participation in the Vietnam War. After having served in Korea as the Assistant Commander, I Corps (Group) Artillery, General Collins had two tours of duty in Vietnam that involved close liaison with all nations participating in the allied effort. In 1964 he was assigned as the senior U.S. adviser to the Vietnamese Regional Forces and Popular Forces, and in May 1965 was named Special Assistant to the Commander, U.S. Military Assistance Command, Vietnam. In the latter capacity General Collins was the personal representative of General Westmoreland to the Vietnamese Joint General Staff on all matters pertaining to the co-ordination of U.S., Vietnamese, and allied forces operations. For his outstanding service in Vietnam, the Republic of Vietnam awarded him the National Order and the Army Distinguished Service Medal, two of its most coveted awards.

Washington, D.C.
15 April 1974

VERNE L. BOWERS
Major General, USA
The Adjutant General

Preface

In 1954 the Army of South Vietnam was a collection of former French colonial troops with little command experience and no support forces worthy of mention. Gradually and despite a considerable degree of political and social instability, the Army, with strong American assistance, was molded into an effective fighting force by the efforts of Vietnamese leaders. After 1960 the South Vietnamese Army also acquired a counterinsurgency capability, but by 1965 increased political turmoil had undermined its effectiveness and necessitated the intervention of strong U.S. combat forces.

From 1965 to 1968, while U.S. forces bore the brunt of the fighting, the South Vietnamese slowly regrouped and, with increasing American advisory assistance and matériel support, once again became an effective fighting force. During this period the military provided security for the civilian population and administration and, in schools and training centers, laid the basis for a larger and more responsive military force.

The battles of the *Tet* offensive of 1968 were followed by the general mobilization of South Vietnam and, one year later, by the decision of the United States to begin troop redeployments. These moves set the stage for the third phase in the Army's development, Vietnamization. The years from 1968 to 1972 saw a great expansion of South Vietnam's territorial security forces and militia, and the continual improvement and modernization of the regular Army as it once again assumed complete responsibility for the war effort.

This monograph, covering the three stages in the growth and development of the South Vietnamese Army, highlights the role of the U.S. Army, especially the MACV advisory system. Most of the material presented is based on official historical summaries prepared on a regular basis by the major U.S. military commands in South Vietnam. Special attention is given to the expansion of South Vietnam's training base and her increasingly sophisticated military school system. While such a study can do no more than survey these activities, it does reflect the deep and continuous commitment by thousands of American soldiers to make the South Vietnamese Army a self-sufficient force capable of defending itself with minimum outside assistance.

Washington, D.C.
15 April 1974

JAMES LAWTON COLLINS, JR.
Brigadier General, U.S. Army

Contents

Chapter	Page
I. THE FORMATIVE YEARS, 1950–1959	1
Background	1
Military Assistance Advisory Group, Vietnam	2
Organization and Force Structure	8
Training	12
II. THE CRUCIAL YEARS, 1960–1964	17
The Problem, 1959–1960	17
The Immediate Response, 1960–1961	18
Counterinsurgency Plan, 1961	20
Presidential Support	21
U.S. Buildup, 1961–1962	25
Establishment of the Military Assistance Command, Vietnam	27
Years of Progress, 1962–1963	29
Years of Crisis, 1963–1964	30
Training of the South Vietnamese Army, 1960–1964	33
Air Support	36
Role of the U.S. Army Special Forces	38
The Civilian Irregular Defense Group Program	40
Territorial Forces: Civil Guard and Self-Defense Corps	41
Civil Affairs	43
III. THE BUILDUP YEARS, 1965–1967	47
Background	47
Military Assistance Command Advisory Expansion	48
U.S. Army Special Forces Advisory Programs	53
Financial Support	55
Manpower Resources	56
The Desertion Problem	60
Economic and Social Improvement	63
Force Structure Expansion	65
Limits of Expansion	67
Territorial Forces	71
The Civilian Irregular Defense Group	74

Chapter	Page
Training and Leadership	75
Offshore Training	79
South Vietnam Schools	80

IV. VIETNAMIZATION, 1968–1972 85

Background	85
Mobilization	85
Force Structure	86
Desertions	91
Pay and Allowances	93
Veteran Affairs	94
Leadership	97
Matériel	100
Training Overview	103
School and Training Center Improvements	105
Combined Arms Training	109
Middle Management Training	110
Advanced Technical Training	111
Pilot Training for the South Vietnam Air Force	112
On-the-Job Training	114
Combined Operations	117
Mobile Advisory Teams	119

V. OVERVIEW 123

General	123
Training Centers	123
Unit Training	126
Military Schools	126
Summary and Conclusions	127

Appendix

A. Major RVNAF Schools and Training Centers Existing at the End of 1958	131
B. RVNAF Academies, Colleges, and Schools	132
C. RVNAF Training School Enrollments for 1970	150
D. Republic of Vietnam Armed Forces	151
GLOSSARY	153
INDEX	155

Maps

No.

1. Location of RVNAF Academies, Colleges, and Schools, 1969	81
2. Location of RVNAF Training Centers, December 1971	107

Illustrations

	Page
U.S. Military Advisory Group Headquarters, Saigon	3
Civil Guard Basic Training Class	11
Officer Candidates Train at Thu Duc	15
U.S. Army Adviser Trains at Battalion Level	25
U.S. Army Aviation Supports South Vietnamese Units	26
Lonely Outpost of Self-Defense Corps	31
CIDG Unit Training	41
New Territorial Recruits	57
Training at Phu Cat	77
Range Practice With New M16 Rifle	78
Cadets at Dalat	82
Rangers Defend Saigon, *Tet*	87
Instruction at Da Nang Vocational School	96
Maintenance Classes for New Equipment	103
Bridge Construction Training, Engineer School	112
Students at Vung Tau Signal School	113
Vietnamese Student Pilots, Ft. Stewart, Ga.	114
Signal Training for Vietnamese	115
MAT Adviser Examines Homemade PF Mortar	121
South Vietnamese Armor in Cambodia	129
South Vietnamese Field Operation	130

All illustrations are from Department of Defense files.

THE DEVELOPMENT AND TRAINING
OF THE SOUTH VIETNAMESE ARMY
1950–1972

CHAPTER I

The Formative Years, 1950–1959

Background

The history of formal U.S. aid to Vietnam began on 1 May 1950, when President Harry S. Truman approved a $10 million grant for urgently needed military assistance items for Indochina. Later, in December, the United States signed a Pentalateral Agreement with France and the associated states of Laos, Cambodia, and Vietnam termed the Mutual Defense Assistance Program. Under this program the U.S. government committed itself to furnish military supplies, material, and equipment to Indochina for the purpose of halting the expansion of communism, and an American Military Assistance Advisory Group (MAAG), Indochina, was formed to administer the support program. From 1950 to 1954 the United States contributed about $1.1 billion to France for the prosecution of the war including some $746 million worth of Army matériel delivered directly to the French Expeditionary Corps in Indochina. However, despite the magnitude of this aid, U.S. advisers exercised little if any supervisory authority. U.S. supplies and equipment were generally turned over to the French, and, until 1955, Military Assistance Advisory Group, Indochina, functioned only as a small logistical accounting group.

Following the Indochina cease-fire agreement (Geneva Accords) of 20 July 1954, the United States became directly involved with advising and assisting the government of Vietnam (south), headed by President Ngo Dinh Diem. The Geneva Accords, a joint agreement between France and the Democratic Republic of Vietnam (north), divided Vietnam at the 17th parallel, provided for the withdrawal of all Communist forces from the south, and established strict limitations and prohibitions on the introduction of foreign military personnel and matériel. Its provisions would be supervised by an International Control Commission (ICC) consisting of representatives from Canada, India, and Poland. The Eisenhower administration regarded the provisions as potentially disastrous and the United States did not sign or endorse the Accords. On 15 June 1954 Lieutenant General John W. "Iron Mike" O'Daniel, chief of Military Assistance Advisory Group, Indochina, had obtained agreement from the French commander in chief for

U.S. participation in training Vietnamese units and requested that more men be sent immediately. After the cease-fire General O'Daniel drew up plans for a comprehensive assistance program for the Army of the Republic of (South) Vietnam, but the U.S. Joint Chiefs of Staff were more cautious and declared it "hopeless to expect a U.S. military training mission to achieve success unless the nation considered is able effectively to perform those governmental functions essential to the successful raising and maintenance of armed forces." In opposition to this view, Secretary of State John Foster Dulles underlined the need "to bolster that government by strengthening the army which supports it." Dulles was backed up by the National Security Council, and in the end political considerations overrode military objections; shortly thereafter Military Assistance Advisory Group, Vietnam, assumed a new training mission in support of the Diem regime. On 22 October 1954 U.S. Ambassador Donald R. Heath and O'Daniel were authorized to "collaborate in setting in motion a crash program designed to bring about an improvement in the loyalty and effectiveness of the Free Vietnamese Forces," and General J. Lawton Collins was sent as a special envoy to Saigon to co-ordinate the endeavor. The result was a formal agreement in December between representatives of France, the Republic of Vietnam, and the United States to supply direct aid through the Military Assistance Program (MAP).

Military Assistance Advisory Group, Vietnam

Shortly after the Geneva Accords the Military Assistance Advisory Group, Indochina, was split into separate components for Vietnam and Cambodia. The former, Military Assistance Advisory Group, Vietnam (MAAGV) (officially designated as such only in October 1955), was limited by the Accords to 342 individuals. With these few the advisory group had the immense task of raising the military capabilities of the Republic of Vietnam armed forces through planning, developing, and administering military assistance. All plans to be co-ordinated with the remaining French forces, and in February 1955 a joint Franco-American Training Relations and Instructions Mission (TRIM) was established with thirty-three U.S. and twenty-eight French officers and enlisted men. Headed by O'Daniel, the Training Relations and Instructions Mission was charged with developing a training program that would deal with Vietnamese command and staff organization and procedures, all planning and logistical activities, and both unit and individual training. To accomplish this mission, the team was

THE U.S. MILITARY ADVISORY GROUP HEADQUARTERS, SAIGON

enlarged and organized in two echelons: a staff that advised and assisted the Vietnamese Ministry of Defense, the Vietnamese General Staff, and the Vietnamese Arms and Service Directorates, and a group of advisers who assisted and advised subordinate headquarters, units, schools, training centers, agencies, and installations. Key staff positions were held by both French and U.S. officers. In the case of the advisory teams, if the senior were French, his immediate assistant was American, and vice versa. These advisory teams were placed within the military geographical subdivisions (regions), the field divisions, light divisions, training centers, and schools. Members of the headquarters staff doubled in duty by acting as advisers to their Vietnamese counterparts in higher headquarters and with the chiefs of the technical services. Since the French still retained a portion of their army in South Vietnam, its chief, General Paul Ely, was technically both head of the Training Relations and Instructions Mission and O'Daniel's operational superior. However, Ely never interfered with TRIM operations, and in the following years the French elements were slowly reduced.

Within this framework the Training Relations and Instructions Mission had two chief objectives: first, to create a conventional army of divisional units and supporting forces by 1 January 1956 and, second, to establish follow-through programs to increase and maintain the efficiency of this force. Furthermore, the combat infantry divisions were to have a dual capability of providing internal security and serving as a blocking or counterattacking force against an external attack. The Training Relations and Instructions Mission set about accomplishing its training objectives through direct relations with the South Vietnamese high command and by the use of mobile training teams consisting of MAAGV personnel and technical service teams which were sent to Vietnam on a temporary duty (TDY) or "loan" status. The use of TDY personnel made it possible to provide increased training support since they were not included in the 342-man MAAGV ceiling imposed by the Accords. Later, on 25 August 1955, the International Control Commission requested that the Military Assistance Advisory Group include all temporary duty personnel in the 342-man ceiling. Instead, the advisory group organized substitute training teams composed of civilian specialists and technicians from the United States and continued its efforts undisturbed. For example, the U.S. Operations Mission (a precursor of the U.S. Agency for International Development) contracted with Michigan State University to provide advisory personnel to the South Vietnam government along with assistance in developing the territorial militia and an effective police organization.

Although the Training Relations and Instructions Mission made some progress in beginning training programs and identifying problem areas, its work was severely limited by the internal military and political situation in South Vietnam. The South Vietnamese Army was still organized into small units and lacked trained leaders, equipment, and adequate logistical capabilities at all levels. These units were scattered throughout the country, and a large proportion of them were still fighting remnants of the religious sects and other factions. The TRIM team continued its existence until the French withdrew their advisers on 28 April 1956. The French continued to maintain a small naval and air advisory mission until the following year.

Throughout the early period a chronic problem of the advisory effort was its lack of personnel. The establishment of a separate Military Assistance Advisory Group for Cambodia in June 1955 and a similar institution, the Programs Evaluation Office, for Laos in December eased the situation somewhat; so also did the transferral of forty-three spaces for administrative support personnel from the U.S. Embassy in Saigon to the Military Assistance Advisory Group in Vietnam in 1957.

These measures could not begin to remedy the basic problem. The background of the situation is fairly clear, but deserves a detailed presentation. At the close of the Indochina War the French Expeditionary Corps had a strength of approximately 140,000. It was agreed at the time of the signing of the defense agreement in December 1954 that the United States would support a reduced Vietnamese armed forces of approximately 100,000. By mid-1955 the French Expeditionary Corps had been reduced to roughly 35,000, and other factors, such as the failure of special representatives of the French and Vietnamese to open negotiations on the future status of the French forces in Vietnam, plus the fact that the French military budget for calendar year 1956 made no provisions for Indochina, indicated a questionable future for the French in Vietnam at best.

A second problem grew out of the dominance of the French in the field of logistics up to 1956. Until that time both Vietnamese and Americans had been excluded from this area, despite the fact that logistical autonomy had been planned for the Vietnamese forces by January 1956. U.S. influence on the logistics system was thus confined to the combined staff efforts of the Training Relations and Instructions Mission and, in actuality, American influence on logistical matters was practically nil. As a result, the Vietnamese in late 1955 were unprepared to assume logistical responsibility for their army, and the limited number of U.S. logistical advisers could do little to offset the lack of Vietnamese experience.

After January 1956 the accelerated withdrawal of the French forces further aggravated an already complex situation. The French literally dumped mountains of equipment upon the Vietnamese. Most of this matériel was improperly packed, indiscriminately piled, often placed in outside storage, and controlled by inadequate or meaningless inventory records. To add to this confusion, the Vietnamese were prone to open all packages to ascertain their contents. It is questionable whether the Vietnamese could have handled this situation properly even if they had been better trained.

With regard to the quality of the equipment, consideration must again be given to the circumstances of the French withdrawal. The French were confronted with a rapidly deteriorating situation in North Africa, which required increasing quantities of personnel and equipment. Therefore, they were primarily concerned with salvaging the best equipment for their own use. With this end in mind, the French were able to exploit the agreement which authorized their removal of MAP-type equipment based on a proportionate input. In the face of French reluctance to allow U.S. personnel to inventory this matériel, there was no way to determine the quality or quantity of equipment.

French refusal to allow U.S. personnel into their installations and dumps covered their natural effort to obtain the best of everything in the quantities desired for their future needs. As a matter of fact, the equipment turned over to the Vietnamese was in both respects inadequate. In most instances, it had been used prior to Indochina and had subsequently seen hard service under wartime conditions. Maintenance requirements could not be met since critical spare parts and tools were nonexistent.

Provisions of the Geneva Accords relating to the introduction of war matériel was also a matter of concern. The French–North Vietnamese protocol specifically defined the nature of "arms, munitions, and war matériel" and also outlined the procedures for the control of the importation and exportation of these items under the supervision and auspices of the International Control Commission. The Accords also established the procedures for notifying the commission in order that credit could be obtained for items exported. However, these provisions were never strictly adhered to. Upon withdrawal, the French took vast quantities of matériel with them. Despite their responsibilities with respect to the Accords, it was assumed that only a small portion of these supplies was reported to the commission in such a way as to obtain credit against future imports. Moreover, because the protocol was concluded between the French and the North Vietnamese, the Saigon government consistently refused to recognize its validity or to comply openly with its provisions. The French were expected to support this position in a showdown since it could be shown that they were remiss in complying with the provisions concerning exportation.

Finally, the Army of the Republic of Vietnam was never reduced to a force goal of 100,000. In light of the rapid withdrawal of most of the French forces, continued Viet Cong buildup, and the civil war against the dissident sect forces, Military Assistance Advisory Group, Vietnam, took the position that such a force goal was inadequate. With the concurrence of the U.S. Embassy in May 1955, the advisory group proposed a 150,000-man force goal to be reached by 1 July 1956, and this proposal was subsequently approved. However, all these developments together with the departure of the French Expeditionary Corps in April 1956 and the dissolution of the Training Relations and Instructions

Mission made it mandatory that U.S. advisory forces be increased.

In order to satisfy this need, the manpower ceilings were bypassed with the establishment of the Temporary Equipment Recovery Mission (TERM) on 1 June 1956. With an authorized strength of 350, the recovery mission raised the total size of Military Assistance Advisory Group, Vietnam, to 692. Overtly the recovery mission was to assist the advisory group in recovering excess war matériel being turned in. In performing this function, the group supervised the removal of large quantities of matériel through exportation, destruction, and scrapping; additional items were sent out of the country for repair and rebuilding and then returned to Vietnam. However, the Temporary Equipment Recovery Mission's real assignment was to aid in developing an adequate and effective South Vietnamese logistical system. TERM personnel were assigned to all major South Vietnamese armed forces logistical organizations. Under their guidance, training courses were developed, selected logistical officers were sent to U.S. service schools, and U.S. supply and maintenance procedures were adopted. Marked progress was realized in the reorganization of the medical, quartermaster, ordnance, and engineer services. Transportation and signal services did not show the same degree of advancement owing to reluctance of certain South Vietnamese Army officers to accept advice and to the lack of trained personnel. But by 1957 the transformation of the logistical facilities had largely been completed, and all the technical services were using U.S. supply procedures. The Temporary Equipment Recovery Mission had been introduced into South Vietnam without official ICC sanction, and in December 1958 the International Control Commission adopted a resolution urging the recovery mission to complete its activities by 30 June 1959. Consultations at the diplomatic level with the Indian ICC representatives extended the completion date to the end of 1960. But the major goal of the United States was to have the size of the Military Assistance Advisory Group in Vietnam legally increased to 888, the total of U.S. and French advisers in South Vietnam at the time of the Geneva Accords. The Canadians were enthusiastic and the U.S. Ambassador requested that the State Department begin immediate negotiations with Ottawa to increase the MAAGV strength ceiling. The dissolution of the Temporary Recovery Mission in 1960 only emphasized the need for more people.

In December 1959 the Office of the Secretary of Defense directed the U.S. Pacific Command (PACOM) to prepare a new MAAGV joint table of distribution to reflect the phase-out of the recovery mission, and in April 1960 the chief of the advisory group indicated that the International Control Commission had favorably considered a request to increase MAAGV strength to 685. On 5 May 1960 the U.S. government officially announced that at the request of the government of South Vietnam the U.S. MAAGV strength would be increased from 327 to 685 members. Implementation of this increase involved the conversion of TERM personnel to MAAGV status during the remainder of 1960.

Organization and Force Structure

Organization and training of the Army of the Republic of Vietnam was the primary task of the Military Assistance Advisory Group, Vietnam, during 1956–59. The South Vietnamese Army had been created in 1949 out of units that had been native auxiliaries to the French Union Forces; these units were commanded by French officers and fought alongside regular French Army units. A series of decrees by the government of Bao Dai, recognized by the French as Supreme Commander of the Armed Forces of the new State of Vietnam, provided a judicial basis for the evolving armed forces. A Ministry of National Defense headed by a Secretary of State for National Defense was established on 19 September 1949. A Vietnamese Air Force was authorized on 25 June 1951, a Vietnamese Navy on 6 March 1952, and a Marine Corps by decree of 13 October 1954.

The earliest MAP support levels provided for a force of 150,000 starting on 1 July 1956. This level had been recommended after determination by the Country Team that the security of the Republic of Vietnam was threatened by both internal subversion and external aggression.[1] However, despite the threat of subversion, initially no provisions were made to provide MAP funding for the paramilitary territorial forces, the Civil Guard, and the Self-Defense Corps militia. Realizing the importance of these paramilitary forces in assuming internal security duties, in November 1956 Military Assistance Advisory Group, Vietnam, recommended that MAP support be provided for a Civil Guard force of 59,000 and a Self-Defense Corps force of 60,000. But it was not until 1961 that any appreciable financial support was available for the paramilitary forces.

At the time of the 1954 armistice, the Vietnamese armed forces numbered about 205,000 men and consisted primarily of infantry

---

[1] The Country Team consisted of the U.S. Ambassador in Saigon, the chief of Military Assistance Advisory Group, and other senior officials who drew up a planning document that dealt with the political, military, economic, and psychological requirements for fighting the Communist insurgency.

units under French officer and noncommissioned officer cadres. This force included 152 infantry battalions, 2 airborne battalions, 2 imperial guard battalions, 2 highlander infantry battalions, 2 armored cavalry squadrons, 6 artillery battalions, and 5 engineer battalions. Under TRIM guidelines these units were reorganized into four standard field divisions of 8,100 men each and six light divisions of 5,800 men each and a number of territorial regiments. The air and sea elements were smaller, ill-equipped, and poorly trained.

Following the June 1954 cease-fire, and the subsequent division of the country, Army strength decreased rapidly. The primary cause was a high desertion rate during the redeployment of troops from North to South Vietnam. During the reorganization period, French officers and noncommissioned officers were withdrawn, and a lightly armed auxiliary force was inactivated. Army strength decreased even more sharply after 1954, while navy and air force strength gradually increased. The armed forces as a whole, however, remained below the 150,000 level supported by the United States.

From 1957 to 1959 the South Vietnamese Army was further restructured under MAAGV guidance to meet the threat of external attack. In October 1957 the advisory group began tests to determine the most effective and practical organization for a standard division. The next two years saw more than two hundred tables of organization and equipment and tables of distribution developed in the search for the proper organization. By September 1959 the South Vietnamese Army had been organized into seven standard divisions of 10,450 men each and three Army corps headquarters. Each division consisted of three infantry regiments, an artillery, a mortar, and an engineer battalion, and company-size support elements. The airborne troops were organized into a five-battalion group and the armor branch into four armored cavalry "regiments" (approximately the equivalent of a U.S. Army cavalry squadron), each containing one squadron (U.S. troop) of M24 light tanks and two squadrons of M8 self-propelled 75-mm. howitzers. The eight independent artillery battalions were equipped with U.S. 10-mm. and 15-mm. pieces. Tactical control was divided between I Corps at Da Nang for the northern and central areas, II Corps at Pleiku for the Central Highlands provinces, and III Corps at Saigon for the southern part of the country. Saigon city remained a special military district.

Throughout this period the paramilitary Civil Guard and Self-Defense Corps remained poor cousins of the regular Army. The Civil Guard had been created by presidential decree in April 1955 from members of inactivated wartime paramilitary agencies and numbered some 68,000 at the end of 1956. Its primary function was to relieve the regular forces of internal security duties, with additional missions of local intelligence collection and countersubversion. The Civil Guard was initially under the direct control of the President, but in September 1958 it was placed under the control of the Ministry of the Interior. Organized into companies and platoons, the Civil Guard was represented by two to eight companies in each province. In addition, eight mobile battalions of 500 men each were controlled from a central headquarters in Saigon and employed in general support mission.

The Self-Defense Corps had existed locally since 1955. It was officially established in April 1956 with some 48,000 nonuniformed troops armed with French weapons. The Self-Defense Corps, like the Civil Guard, was established to free regular forces from internal security duties by providing a police organization at village level to protect the population from subversion and intimidation. Units of four to ten men each were organized in villages of 1,000 or more inhabitants. The chain of command extended from the Ministry of the Interior to the province chiefs, district chiefs, and village councils. The Civil Guard and the Self-Defense Corps were poorly trained and ill-equipped to perform their missions, and by 1959 their numbers had declined to about 46,000 and 40,000, respectively.

Command and control of the South Vietnamese defense forces was less than satisfactory. President Diem appointed the Secretary of State for National Defense who in turn supervised the activities of the General Staff chief and several special subdepartments. The General staff chief, in turn, supervised the Army staff and, through it, the military regions and the field commands. In practice the system was beset by conflicting, duplicating channels of command and communications and by duplicate offices or agencies with overlapping interests. To further complicate matters, various major agencies of the Department of National Defense were installed in widely separated areas, so as to hamper co-ordination, rapid staff action, and decision-making.

Problems resulting from this command structure were frequent. Often a division commander would receive orders from both the corps commander (who should have been his undisputed boss) and the region commander in whose region his division was stationed. In another case, branch (infantry, armor, and so forth) chiefs would give orders to units of their branches while the units in question were assigned to field commands. Perhaps the most flagrant case involved the President himself, who, using his radio

CIVIL GUARD BASIC TRAINING CLASS

net from a van in the garden of the presidential palace, sometimes sent out operational orders directly to combat regiments, bypassing the Department of National Defense, the General Staff, and the field commands. An example of duplicate agencies of primary interest was the presence of a Director of Air Technical Service (who was nominally directly under the Chief of the Armed Forces General Staff but actually subordinate to the Director General of Administration, Budget, and Comptroller for fiscal matters) and a Deputy Chief of Air Staff for Matériel.

The physical location of various agencies also caused problems. The Department of National Defense and most of the central organizations and the ministerial services were located in downtown Saigon, while the General Staff (less air and navy elements) was inefficiently located in a series of company-size troop barracks on the edge of the city. The chief of the General Staff was thus removed several miles from the Department of National Defense. The navy and air staffs were also separately located in downtown Saigon. With such a physical layout, staff action and decision-making unduly delayed on even the simplest of matters.

The over-all ministerial structure described above was originally set up by the French and slightly modified by presidential decree on 3 October 1957. Military Assistance Advisory Group, Vietnam, had proposed a different command structure which would have placed the ministry and the "general staff" in closer proximity both physically and in command relationship. But the proposal was not accepted by President Diem, perhaps because he wished to continue to maintain a division of power and prevent any one individual—other than himself—from having too much authority. Thus, during the period in question, the existing system was accepted by the advisory group which, in turn, served as lubrication for its more delicate components.

Training

In organizing and training the South Vietnamese Army, the United States relied heavily on its recent experience in South Korea. The similarity between the Vietnamese situation of 1954 and the Korean situation of 1950 prompted the Military Assistance Advisory Group in Vietnam to concentrate on developing a South Vietnamese force capable of meeting an overt invasion from North Vietnam. While the threat of an external aggression was real, it was not until 1959 that the internal subversion and insurgency openly supported by the north was recognized as the major threat and that a strong effort to give South Vietnam a counterinsurgency capability began.

Troops for the armed forces were obtained through voluntary enlistments and conscription. The military service law enacted 29 June 1953 prescribed a continuing active and reserve obligation for all male citizens between the ages of eighteen and forty-five. Under the conscription program, initiated on 1 August 1957 and amended in January 1959, male citizens aged twenty and twenty-one were called up for an eighteen-month service period. In addition, preinduction training was given in high schools to physically fit males fifteen years of age or older. Graduates of this two-year compulsory training program received no military rank, but if they were later inducted they were often sent to officer candidate school.

During this period, South Vietnamese trainees underwent a 31-week training program that had been developed by modifying appropriate U.S. Army training programs to conform to Vietnamese requirements. As in the United States, the training cycle consisted of four phases: basic individual, advanced individual, basic unit, and advanced unit training. To assist in the massive training process U.S. Army field manuals were translated, and both mobile training and contract civilian teams were active, despite ICC objections. One such team, consisting of personnel from the 1st U.S. Army Special Forces Group (Airborne), conducted a sixteen-week course at the Commando Training Center at Nha Trang. For the most part the South Vietnamese Army fully utilized these teams, although at times U.S. methods were adopted only with reluctance.

The Military Assistance Advisory Group in Vietnam had hoped to have all tactical units complete a full cycle of training by the end of 1957, but progress was slow. Initial plans had called for the Civil Guard and the Self-Defense Corps to take over the internal security mission while the South Vietnamese Army was undergoing training. But, since the poorly trained and ill-equipped paramilitary forces were unable to fulfill this task, it was continually necessary to divert regular forces away from their training program for operational requirements. Hoping to correct this deficiency, the advisory group established provincial training centers to provide at least four weeks of instruction to Civil Guard and Self-Defense Corps personnel. Although this step helped the situation somewhat, by mid-1958 three divisions, the airborne group, a majority of the combat engineers, and all of the territorial regiments had had either major interruptions or no training at all because of operational demands.

Despite delays, the advisory group began an expanded training program in 1958. The new program was to proceed in two cycles: 1) a six-phase cycle of thirty-two weeks leading to advanced unit training and concluding with field maneuvers at regimental level and 2) followed by an annual training cycle of fifty-two weeks within each corps area. The 32- and 52-week training programs extended to all arms and services and were based on modified U.S. Army training programs. The goal continued to be the construction of a conventional military force, and by September 1959 the training picture had brightened. Two of the seven infantry divisions were in the advanced unit training phase, as were the airborne group and the five general reserve artillery battalions. The engineer groups were in on-the-job training and building roads and bridges stage, and considerable progress had been made in training combat and service support elements. In order to emphasize realistic tactical field training, two divisions were scheduled to participate in maneuvers in January 1960, and night combat training was increased throughout all phases of instruction.

Concurrent with the expansion and improvement in the tactical training programs, the Military Assistance Advisory Group devoted considerable effort to the development of a South Vietnamese Army service school and training system. The French military school system in Indochina reflected its own metropolitan system, but was modified significantly by the practice of never promoting native personnel into positions higher than junior officer. As a result, Vietnamese officers were usually untrained for command and staff positions higher than company level. As early as October 1956, MAAGV personnel participated with key Vietnamese officers on a master school planning board. The board gathered factual information on all schools as a basis for developing a master plan and directed key changes in organizations and location. An Army school system was started to provide technical and specialist schools, arm and service basic and advanced courses, a military academy to train select young men for commissions in the Army, and a replacement training center to provide basic training for conscripts and new enlistees. The system was built around six key centers:

1. a general school center at Thu Duc with a capacity for 1,000 students and comprising most of the arm and service technical and specialist schools;

2. a separate infantry school, to be located initially also at Thu Duc, which would include a 400-student officer candidate school and later basic branch officer and noncommissioned officer courses;

3. medical, intelligence, and psychological warfare schools to be located in the Saigon area owing to the availability of facilities and other resources;

4. the Military Academy at Dalat, with a two-year curriculum combining academic and military subjects to train new officers, to be transformed later into a four-year institution;

5. a higher military school or college, located in Saigon with a capacity of 250 students; and

6. a centralized replacement camp for training conscripts located at Quang Trung near Saigon and with an annual capacity of approximately 24,000 (or about 8,000 at any one time).

In practice, the principal training establishment during this period was the Quang Trung Training Center, near Saigon, which gave eight weeks of basic training to all recruits and which gave advanced courses to infantry soldiers. Training in other branches of service was given at the specialized training centers, especially those at the Thu Duc Military Schools Center. Regular officers were trained at the Military Academy at Dalat and received further career schooling at the Thu Duc Military Schools complex, at the Command and General Staff College in Saigon, and in schools abroad. Many reserve officers, obligated to serve two years, passed through the Officer Candidate School at Thu Duc. The continued development of the school system made it possible to reduce the number of personnel which had to be sent every year for specialized and advanced training, or at least it made this type of training more selective.

By the end of 1958 a total of eighteen schools and training cen-

OFFICER CANDIDATES TRAIN AT THU DUC

ters had been established and were training about 20,000 a year. *(See Appendixes A and B.)* Another important addition was an expanded English Language School. Finally, unit schools conducted training in such subjects as leadership, communications, and automotive operations.

Another vital link in the American training effort was the Off-Shore School Program. Begun in 1955 under MAP sponsorship, it provided formal training for both officer and enlisted men in all branches of the Army at CONUS (continental United States) and overseas U.S. Army schools and included orientation tours for senior officers at various U.S. installations. The importance of this program soon became evident. During the French era in Vietnam all key command and staff positions had been occupied by French officers. After 1954 many Vietnamese officers had to occupy positions for which they had insufficient training experience. This situation was particularly critical in the technical and logistical areas. By fiscal year 1954 a total of 3,644 Vietnamese officers and enlisted men were trained under the Off-Shore School Program in CONUS installations and schools, and 726 were trained at overseas Army installations. This program was highly successful in training key Vietnamese officers and specialists, but needed to be expanded. The fiscal year 1960 Military Assistance Program therefore provided for the training of 1,375 Vietnamese soldiers in the United States and 226 in allied countries. Probably the most valid criticism was U.S. development of the South Vietnamese Army into a conventional military force not properly organized, equipped, and trained to contest the guerrilla in the jungles and mountains where he lurks. The realization came in 1959 and massive efforts were finally begun to train Vietnamese units and personnel in counterinsurgency warfare. But owing in part to the strength of the South Vietnamese Army, there was no conventional attack from North Vietnam similar to the invasion of South Korea.

The obstacles Americans faced in training the Vietnamese during this early period were many. Some were overcome. MAAGV advisers noted critical training deficiencies, with incomplete unit training heading the list. Rising operational requirements made it impossible to institute effective training exercises for units already constituted—a shortcoming for which harder or longer training for the individual recruit could not compensate. One result was the distinct lack of knowledge of techniques in combined arms operations and amphibious and other joint operations. Officers at all levels lacked the experience and military schooling needed to qualify them for their positions. Another serious problem was the shortage of officers and enlisted specialists for the technical services. Units and schools both suffered from a shortage of trained instructors. Finally, despite all efforts, the output of Vietnamese proficient in the English language never met the increasing demand for this most difficult skill.

Although progress had been made in years past in training and organizing the Republic of Vietnam armed forces, the internal situation in South Vietnam had deteriorated to the point that the Viet Cong were gradually gaining the initiative. By 1959 the enemy had greatly increased the tempo of his activities, ambushing and attacking large military installations. Despite these developments, both the MAAGV chief, Lieutenant General Samuel T. Williams, and the U.S. Ambassador remained optimistic. As late as the spring of 1960 Williams was convinced that Saigon was in no danger and that a phased withdrawal of the Military Assistance Advisory Group in Vietnam could begin soon. In retrospect, his judgments were to appear premature.

CHAPTER II

The Crucial Years, 1960–1964

The Problem, 1959–1960

By 1960 it was apparent that the armed forces of the Republic of Vietnam were incapable of dealing with the growing insurgency. Since 1956 the Viet Cong had been slowly turning the south into a battlefield of unconventional warfare and eroding the limited authority of Saigon in the countryside. Assassinations and other acts of terrorism began to rise rapidly and for the first time battalion-size attacks occurred against isolated posts and small towns. When, on 26 January 1960, the Viet Cong overran a South Vietnamese Army regimental headquarters in Tay Ninh Province and captured large amounts of arms and ammunition, U.S. planners realized that new and forceful actions and programs were needed if the government of Vietnam was to survive. The coming years would be crucial.

The United States had already begun responding to this new threat. The previous year, in May 1959, the Commander in Chief, Pacific (CINCPAC), directed that MAAGV advisers be provided down to infantry regiment and to artillery, armored, and separate Marine battalion level. This move would enable advisers to give on-the-spot advice and effectively assess the end result of the advisory effort. The Pacific commander in chief's orders forbade the advisers to participate directly in combat operations or to accompany units on antiguerrilla operations immediately adjacent to national boundaries. The Commander in Chief, Pacific, also took steps to obtain U.S. Army Special Forces mobile training teams to assist in training indigenous "Ranger" companies for counterguerrilla warfare. The Ranger units had been created by President Diem, against U.S. advice, simply by taking the fourth company out of each infantry battalion and redesignating it. These Ranger units thus constituted a special branch of the Army—in addition to the Vietnamese Special Forces—but as yet had received no special training which would justify their new mission.

The major elements of the Republic of Vietnam armed forces at this time were three corps headquarters, seven infantry divisions, one airborne brigade, the Ranger force of about 9,000 men, three Marine battalions, a token Air Force and Navy, and a small number of logistical support units. In 1960 the Military Assistance Advisory Group reported that the Republic of Vietnam armed forces were about 13,000 below its authorized 150,000 level and that both the Civil Guard and the Self-Defense Corps were below strength and still largely untrained. The Civil Guard and the Self-Defense Corps were not considered part of the Republic of Vietnam Army or armed forces until 1964. MAP support was available for about 25,000 Civil Guardsmen, but the Self-Defense Corps was still not receiving any financial aid. In view of the growing insurgency these force levels had to be raised and both the training program and the organization of the Army modified to provide the armed forces with a greatly strengthened counterinsurgency capability.

At the Pacific commanders conference in April 1959 General Williams, the chief of Military Assistance Advisory Group, Vietnam, reviewed the situation in Vietnam and cited what he felt were the most serious problems: absence of a national plan for control of the situation, no rotation of military units in the field, the need for a central surveillance plan, the proliferation of Ranger-type counterinsurgency units, the lack of intelligence concerning enemy activities, an inadequate military communications system, and the need for a single commander to direct the war effort. Williams also underlined the inability of the Civil Guard to maintain internal security and the ensuing commitment of South Vietnam Army units to stability operations in lieu of training. The Civil Guard was still under the government of Vietnam's Department of Interior and controlled locally by the province and district chiefs. While this arrangement made it possible for the U.S. Operations Mission to support the Civil Guard financially, it also made it extremely difficult to implement any significant improvements for these scattered troops.

The Immediate Response, 1960–1961

In March 1960 the U.S. Joint Chiefs of Staff (JCS) began drawing up a comprehensive counterinsurgency plan which would unite all U.S. and South Vietnamese elements behind a common objective. At the same time, the Joint Chiefs reversed their past policy and recommended that the Vietnamese Army develop a counterinsurgency capability over and above that supplied by the territorials. Later, in June, the Military Assistance Advisory Group approved the formation of several Ranger battalions to spearhead the counterinsurgency effort, and in September the advisory group, under its new chief, Lieutenant General Lionel C. McGarr, supervised the development of the new counterinsurgency plan at the Saigon level. Finally, in October, the advisory group recommended an immediate 20,000-man increase in the South Vietnamese armed forces structure.

Efforts to restructure the expanded Vietnamese Army and armed forces for the counterinsurgency effort had only mixed success. In March 1960 the government of Vietnam approved in principle a national planning system without providing for the necessary national level direction and control to ensure that the system would be implemented and integrated.

Although the chief of the South Vietnam armed forces Joint General Staff (JGS) received responsibility for the military security of the nation, the tools necessary to fulfill this responsibility were either denied him or were made ineffective. Individuals and agencies not directly or fully responsible to the Joint General Staff still had direct influence over units and agencies of the South Vietnam armed forces. For example, forty-two key leaders, each responsible for pacification within his own sphere of responsibility, reported directly to President Diem. These included the thirty-eight province chiefs who by-passed all military authority, three military region commanders who by-passed the Joint General Staff and field commands, and one field commander. President Diem remained reluctant to delegate responsibility or to furnish the means to individuals whereby they might accomplish their missions and insisted on retaining tight control of all civilian and military activities.

On 7 October 1960 President Diem, at the urging of the U.S. Ambassador, re-established the Internal Security Council to coordinate governmental actions at the highest level. The Internal Security Council would be similar to the U.S. National Security Council and act as an executive agent for Diem by issuing orders and instructions to the Department of National Defense and other government agencies instrumental in carrying out the counterinsurgency campaign. This setup placed responsibility on the Permanent Secretary-General for National Defense for executing council decisions. Later, on 3 December, a South Vietnam government decree placed the Civil Guard under the control of the Department of National Defense. This arrangement allowing Military Assistance Advisory Group to assume responsibility for training and equipping the Civil Guard, with the cost to be borne by the International Cooperation Administration, represented a major organizational improvement.

Counterinsurgency Plan, 1961

In August 1960 the U.S. Departments of Defense and State approved the JCS outline plan for counterinsurgency operations in Vietnam and Laos, and the Country Team in South Vietnam proceeded to prepare a more detailed plan based on this initial guidance. The final Counterinsurgency Plan was approved on 6 February 1961 and laid down the basic guidelines for most future U.S. plans and actions. Its objective was to halt the spreading insurgency by reforming and enlarging the military forces of the government of Vietnam. In concept, the plan divided most of the country into tactical control zones supervised by military headquarters of appropriate size and strength. Security would be provided by a combination of regular, Ranger, and territorial units. The Counterinsurgency Plan proposed to raise MAP support for the Vietnamese armed forces from 150,000 men to 170,000 and to support a Civil Guard force of aproximately 68,000. The proposed 20,000-man Army increase was to provide 15,000 spaces for combat forces and 5,000 spaces for logistical support units.

The major increase in the combat forces called for the activation of three infantry regiments (about 7,000 spaces) which would allow the Vietnamese Army to maintain its current field strength. Specific counterinsurgency elements were also strengthened. One-fifth of the increase (about 3,000 spaces) was pledged to expand the Ranger units from sixty-five to eighty-six companies. By this time all sixty-five existing companies had been trained and equipped for counterinsurgency operations and were committed. Equally important, the Vietnamese Special Forces were to be more than tripled with a 500-man increase. These units had been trained by U.S. Army Special Forces teams to carry out unconventional warfare operations behind enemy lines and by early 1961 were being employed to conduct long-range reconnaissance operations; search out, organize, and direct anti-Viet Cong elements including ethnic and religious groups; recruit and organize tribal (Montagnard) border watchers; and establish intelligence nets along the Cambodian and Laotian borders. In an attempt to cope with the serious deficiency in military intelligence, the Counterinsurgency Plan proposed establishing the equivalent of a U.S. Army military intelligence battalion. The battalion would include a security company, an intelligence collection company, a linguistic company (interrogator-translator), and cellular intelligence teams designed to support tactical intelligence needs or to conduct co-ordinated operations on an area basis. The unit would thus provide a wide range of intelligence support at all echelons for the equivalent of a field army.

Other major additions included two civil affairs companies, one air support operations center at each corps headquarters, twenty-four air-ground teams to provide better co-ordination for air support, and a CH–34 helicopter squadron to permit the lift of one rifle company. The 5,000 logistical spaces would correct the imbalance in support activities. New support units would be organized, and the logistical system would be restructured to provide regional logistical commands to support the tactical commanders in the field. These changes would end the inherent problems of the existing system that attempted to control all logistical support operations from Saigon.

The Counterinsurgency Plan also strove to strengthen the Joint General Staff by creating a Joint Operations Staff within the Joint General Staff that would have the mission and authority to develop national plans for pacification and other operations. Joint Operations Staff control was to be exercised through subordinate headquarters following normal command channels of the military organization. In addition, the plan visualized that in areas where pacification operations were to be conducted, supreme authority would be vested in a senior tactical military commander. All agencies, both military and civilian, would be subordinated to this commander during the period of operations.

Presidential Support

In April 1961, in response to the deteriorating situation in Southeast Asia, President John F. Kennedy inaugurated a series of actions designed to bolster the Republic of Vietnam and demonstrate to the world his firm determination to take whatever steps were necessary to defend that country. In April representatives of the United States and the Republic of Vietnam signed a treaty of amity and economic relationships, and the National Security Council, with the chief of the Military Assistance Advisory Group, Vietnam, in attendance, took steps to inaugurate a program to assist South Vietnam. A special group, Task Force Vietnam, was formed initially under the Department of Defense to guide the program; later the State Department assumed responsibility. A counterpart body, Task Force Saigon, consisting essentially of the South Vietnam Country Team, was organized to formulate an effective program on the ground level. Although Military Assistance Advisory

Group, Vietnam, was not initially included in Task Force Saigon, it later gained representation.

At this time President Diem abolished the system of military regions and made his army field command responsible for counterinsurgency operations. This step proved relatively ineffective, for President Diem continued to retain tight control of all operations. No single military chain of command from the field command to the units and agencies engaged in counterinsurgency operations existed; corps and military district commanders continued to receive their instructions directly from the President. On 11 May 1961 Vice President Lyndon B. Johnson visited South Vietnam to discuss the matter of increased aid with the Vietnamese officials. One of the conditions for continued U.S. aid was to be a reorganization of the entire political-military setup. President Diem agreed but continued to dominate military operations.

On 13 May 1961 both President Kennedy and Secretary of State Dean Rusk declared that the Republic of Vietnam was to get added military and economic assistance and that consideration was to be given to the use of U.S. forces, if necessary, to help resist internal Communist pressure in Vietnam. This joint communiqué was followed on 19 May by President Kennedy's announcement of his Presidential Action Program. The program approved the basic elements of the MAAGV Counterinsurgency Plan and increased U.S. financial aid by $41 million to support the higher force levels. Specifically, the Presidential Action Program authorized the following measures:

1. MAP support for a 20,000-man increase in the South Vietnam armed forces strength;

2. augmentation of the Military Assistance Advisory Group to ensure effective implementation of the program, to include the training of the additional 20,000 troops;

3. consideration of an increase in the South Vietnam armed forces strength beyond the 170,000 limit;

4. MAP support for the entire Civil Guard force of 68,000 men;

5. expansion of advisory support to the Self-Defense Corps; and

6. provision of more U.S. Special Forces mobile training teams to speed up the training of the Vietnamese Special Forces.

While the Presidential Action Program was being implemented, South Vietnam leaders in mid-June 1961 made their own force level proposals. Their request corresponded closely with an earlier proposal by Military Assistance Advisory Group on 19 May and outlined the creation of a fifteen-division force totaling 278,-000 men. This was to be a phased buildup, and as a first step they requested two divisions requiring an over-all Vietnamese armed forces increase of 30,000. In consideration of the South Vietnam government request, on 4 August President Kennedy announced that the United States would support an armed force of 200,000 men, with the condition that an agreement on the training and employment of these additional 30,000 men be reached. No decision was made on the request for a force increase above the 200,000 level.

At first, these measures had little effect on the situation in the field. Activation of new units created by the force increases was to be completed by the end of 1961. However, by the end of August, Vietnamese armed forces strength was only about 153,000—far short of the 170,000 goal and farther still from an Army of more than 200,000. By September it was thus apparent that the Presidential Action Program was in danger of bogging down. Funds were slow in having an impact, and both desertions and combat operations continued to take a rising toll of available personnel. The creation of new units only stretched existing leadership and personnel resources. Moreover, the government of Vietnam had only barely begun to show receptiveness to U.S. proposals and advice for military reorganization, and the danger of defeat loomed closer than ever. Thus, in October 1961, President Kennedy sent General Maxwell D. Taylor to South Vietnam to make an on-the-spot analysis of the situation and establish the basis for new decisions.

Taylor reported that the South Vietnamese government was losing the war through poor tactics and administration, and he recommended increased American support for the territorial forces, an expansion of Military Assistance Advisory Group, and the introduction of American logistical support forces into Vietnam to increase the mobility of the South Vietnamese Army. During Taylor's visit President Diem had asked for a bilateral defense treaty with the United States and for the dispatch of U.S. combat troops to his country, but in November President Kennedy decided not to commit U.S. forces and instead to bolster the military strength of South Vietnam.

On 4 December 1961, however, President Kennedy informed President Diem that the United States was ready to participate in a sharply increased joint effort with the South Vietnamese government. Referring to a memorandum of understanding previously approved by President Diem, President Kennedy's communication outlined fundamental new steps in U.S.-South Vietnamese collaboration, including the participation of U.S. uniformed troops in operational missions with South Vietnam Army forces and close Vietnamese consultation with American advisers in planning the conduct of security efforts. All forms of aid previously furnished were to be increased significantly. The United States would specifically provide the following:

1. increased airlift to South Vietnamese forces, including helicopters, light aviation and transport aircraft, manned as necessary by U.S. uniformed personnel and under U.S. operational control;

2. additional equipment and personnel required for air reconnaissance, photography, instruction in the execution of air-ground support techniques, and special intelligence;

3. small craft and U.S. uniformed advisers and operating personnel for surveillance and control of coastal and inland waterways;

4. expedited training and equipment for the Civil Guard and Self-Defense Corps to relieve regular forces from static missions and use them for mobile offensive operations;

5. necessary personnel and equipment for improving the military and political intelligence systems, beginning at the province level and extending upward through the government and armed forces; and

6. additional personnel to Military Assistance Advisory Group to support the increased U.S. participation.

The subject received further attention at the Secretary of Defense conference held in Hawaii that December. There Secretary of Defense Robert S. NcNamara authorized Military Assistance Advisory Group to provide an adviser for each province chief and advisory teams down to battalion level for operational units. In order to expedite the training of the Civil Guard and the Self-Defense Corps, new training centers were to be established and adviser strengths increased. In addition, the need for intelligence advisers to improve the marginal intelligence capabilities of the Vietnamese was recognized; these specialists would assist corps, divisions, and province headquarters as well as higher level staffs. At that time, the Secretary of Defense indicated that the existing U.S. policy did not anticipate the employment of American troops against the Viet Cong; however, South Vietnam was to have the highest priority for aid, and the United States was to provide everything needed to control the rising insurgency except combat troops. Secretary McNamara also indicated that money was not to be a controlling consideration in planning operations. Conferees also decided that the United States would prepare detailed campaign plans for submission to the South Vietnam government and to the Vietnamese field commanders, and also a border control plan. All these measures meant more American personnel so that by the end of the year MAAGV strength authorization had again been pushed up.

U.S. Army Adviser Trains at Battalion Level

U.S. Buildup, 1961–1962

The proposed counterinsurgency program placed equal stress on civic, economic, and military actions. Civilian contract technical representatives acted both as instructors and skilled workers; mobile training teams set up courses of instruction for intelligence, chemical, biological, and radiological, and psychological warfare activities. Six Vietnamese Army and nine Civil Guard training centers as well as two divisional training areas were programed for completion by September 1962 to provide for increased training requirements resulting from the South Vietnam armed forces increase of 20,000 men. By September 1961, three Vietnamese Army training centers were in operation and were receiving American personnel to help train three recently activated Vietnamese Army regiments. During 1961 the most important training activities in South Vietnam were the training of Ranger units, the Civil Guards and the Self-Defense Corps; the use of the mobile training teams; the establishment of a medical training center at Saigon; the establishment of a Republic of Vietnam armed forces Joint General Staff Combat Development and Research Center; and the training

SOUTH VIETNAMESE TROOPS BOARDING U.S. ARMY HELICOPTER

of the Vietnamese Junk Force, for which MAP funds were authorized late in 1961.

In mid-1961, the chief of the Republic of Vietnam armed forces Joint General Staff authorized MAAGV advisers to accompany Vietnamese battalion and company-size units in combat with the understanding that they would only observe and advise. This authority, with which the Commander in Chief, Pacific, concurred, was intended to permit advisers to help Vietnamese commanders in operational, signal, and logistical matters; in the establishment and operation of aerial supply points; and in communication advice and support. Although armed, the advisers were not to engage in actual combat except in self-defense.

The expansion of the Vietnamese armed forces, the determination to authorize MAP support for the Civil Guard and Self-Defense Corps, and related training and administrative problems caused a sharp increase in MAAGV strength. The Joint Chiefs of Staff authorized a MAAGV increase from a May 1961 base of 740 personnel, 574 of which were U.S. Army, to 1,904 spaces (to include, 1,606 U.S. Army personnel.) In December 1961 the Commander in Chief, Pacific, requested that the Joint Chiefs augment the MAAGV staff by forty-five to provide an Aviation Section and a Naval Section in the Operation Division. As of 12 December 1961, the actual MAAGV strength was 1,062. In addition, 1,209 military and civilian personnel were present for duty and working directly for Military Assistance Advisory Group, Vietnam, on classified and other miscellaneous projects. Also in December, two helicopter companies (438 men) arrived in South Vietnam.

Most U.S. personnel increases occurred during the last three months of 1961, creating logistical problems that arose primarily from a lack of policy guidance regarding fund resources and support responsibilities. U.S. TOE units deployed to South Vietnam were supported by their parent services. The expansion of the advisory effort involving American personnel and equipment assigned to South Vietnam units in the field committed U.S. men to field communications and intelligence operations and made necessary the assignment of additional U.S. personnel to MAAGV. Some of the equipment involved in the buildup program was to be included in the fiscal year 1962 Military Assistance Program for South Vietnam. Some questions also existed concerning title to other equipment sent in for use by U.S. forces for which the fund source remained undetermined by the end of 1961. These problems, coupled with the arrival of American combat support units, made clear that a single control agency was required to guide the U.S. military effort in the Republic of Vietnam.

Establishment of the Military Assistance Command, Vietnam

On 23 November 1961 the Joint Chiefs of Staff directed the Commander in Chief, Pacific, to be prepared to establish a unified or joint (Army–Navy–Air Force) command and develop a suitable staff for a Commander, U.S. Forces, Vietnam, with the object of increasing U.S. military and economic assistance to the Republic of Vietnam and of increasing American participation in the effort to eliminate the Viet Cong. The Joint Chiefs envisaged that a commander of U.S. forces in Vietnam would control all intelligence operations, all MAAGV functions having a direct bearing on Vietnamese armed forces combat capabilities, and economic aid relating to counterinsurgency. The commander of U.S. forces in Vietnam would have the mission of assisting and supporting South Vietnam in defeating Communist insurgency and in destroying the Viet Cong. He would also have full authority over all U.S. assets in South Vietnam that could or should be used in a unified effort against the Viet Cong, and he would be the principal U.S. military adviser and single spokesman for American military affairs in South Vietnam.

As planned by the Joint Chiefs of Staff, the commander of U.S. forces in Vietnam would have a small joint and special staff to concentrate on planning, operations, and intelligence; a service component was to handle the actual troop support; and the Vietnamese armed forces training advisory function was to remain with Chief, Military Assistance Advisory Group, Vietnam, who would also be the Pacific commander in chief's direct representative in planning, programing, and administering the Military Assistance Program. The Joint Chiefs also wanted a small logistical support activity to be established to back up all elements of the commander of U.S. forces in Vietnam as well as a research and development center and a Joint Unconventional Warfare Task Force (to include Controlled American Source, U.S. Operation Mission, and U.S. Information Service).

On 8 February, with the approval of President Kennedy, Secretary of Defense McNamara, and the Joint Chiefs of Staff, the Commander in Chief, Pacific, Admiral Harry D. Felt, established a U.S. Military Assistance Command, Vietnam (USMACV), and designated Lieutenant General Paul D. Harkins (who was promoted to general) as commander (COMUSMACV). The Commander in Chief, Pacific, also set forth terms of reference for the new command. The Commander, U.S. Military Assistance Command, Vietnam, as the senior U.S. military commander in the Republic of Vietnam, was directly responsible for all U.S. military policy, operations, and assistance in that country. He was authorized to discuss both American and Vietnamese military operations directly with President Diem and other South Vietnam leaders. The MACV commander also had access to the Joint Chiefs of Staff and to the Secretary of Defense through the Pacific commander in chief. However, since the U.S. Ambassador to South Vietnam was responsible for American political and basic policy matters, the MACV commander was to consult with him on those matters. If a difference of view existed, both the MACV commander and the U.S. Ambassador could communicate their positions directly to Washington for decision. Both the U.S. Ambassador and the MACV commander were also responsible for keeping each other fully informed, especially on all high-level contacts with the Republic of Vietnam, major military plans, and pending operations.

Military Assistance Command, Vietnam, was also kept separate from Military Assistance Advisory Group, Vietnam. General Harkins was charged directly with the responsibility for all military policy, operations, and assistance in South Vietnam and for advising the government of Vietnam on all matters relative to security, organization, and use of the regular and paramilitary forces. The Military Assistance Advisory Group remained a separate entity still charged with the mission of training and advising the armed forces, and it was subordinate to Military Assistance Command. On 16 February the Joint Chiefs authorized 216 spaces for the new headquarters which began to function shortly thereafter.

Years of Progress, 1962–1963

By 1962 many of the measures taken during the past two years began to bear fruit. Significant gains were made in all areas owing to the buildup of U.S. advisory and operational support forces, and the greater strength and effectiveness of both the South Vietnam Army and the territorial units. Regular force strength grew to approximately 219,000, exceeding the 200,000 authorized level. The Civil Guard expanded to a total of 77,000 and the Self-Defense Corps to 99,500, and a new paramilitary force, the Civilian Irregular Defense Group (CIDG), was established and, by the end of 1962, totaled about 15,000. In 1963 MAP supported levels rose to 225,000 for the Vietnamese armed forces, 86,000 for the Civil Guard, and 104,000 for the Self-Defense Corps.

Significant organizational changes were also made in 1962. Separate Army, Navy, Air Force, and Special Forces commands were established as major subordinate elements of the armed forces; a Joint Operations Center was created at the JGS level to control military operations of national scope; and South Vietnam was operationally divided into four corps tactical zones (CTZ) and a Capital Military District. A field corp headquarters controlled each corps tactical zone while a special command ran the more sensitive Capital Military District.

Long-range planning activities also intensified during 1962 and resulted in the Comprehensive Plan for South Vietnam. The plan, in intent and purpose, was conceptually an extension of the Counterinsurgency Plan of 1960. Its objective was to provide the government of Vietnam with the military assistance and equipment necessary to bring the insurgency under control, maintain its sovereignty, and allow the United States to phase out special military assistance beginning in 1964. To attain its objectives, the Comprehensive Plan for South Vietnam depended on the success of the development and implementation of the many supporting military plans and programs. Among the most vital were the National Campaign Plan, the Strategic Hamlet Program, and the CIDG Program. Increased military force levels were also critical. The Comprehensive Plan envisaged a peak armed strength of 575,000 in mid-1963 with a gradual phase-down to 368,000 as the government approached its goal of controlling 90 percent of the population.

Long-range plans were also being developed which provided for a decrease in the South Vietnamese armed forces structure over a five-year period and a reduction of 1,000 U.S. personnel. The final plan, called the Accelerated Model Plan, was based on the assumption that the Viet Cong insurgency would be suppressed by the end of 1964 in the northern and central areas and by 1965 in the delta; after that, it was assumed, only a Military Assistance Advisory Group of about 3,000 personnel would be required. These plans were never to be put into effect.

Years of Crisis, 1963–1964

By the end of 1962 it appeared that U.S. efforts had been successful. The buildup of its advisory and operational support strength together with its intense emphasis on counterinsurgency instruction had greatly improved South Vietnamese armed forces operational efficiency, and military trends were beginning to favor South Vietnam. Over-all U.S. military strength had more than tripled during the year and now totaled 11,326, while the MAAGV staff had grown from an authorized strength of 1,949 at the end of 1961 to 2,989 (of which 1,138 were designated as field advisers). But suddenly in 1963 the situation was dramatically reversed and U.S. optimism quickly faded. The Buddhist riots during the summer were only a prelude to the military coup which ousted the Diem regime. This event, in turn, sparked a period of renewed civil unrest and political instability from which the South Vietnam government did not begin to emerge until late 1965. The U.S. advisory and assistance effort was caught in the middle.

General Harkins refused to let his advisers report to their assigned units if those units were to be used to quell Buddhist riots or for other nonmilitary purposes. When Diem declared martial law on 22 August and began mass arrests of Buddhists, a resolution was introduced into the U.S. Senate calling for the withdrawal of all American forces and halting all aid unless the Diem government abandoned its repressive policies. Diem ended martial law on 16 September, but economic aid was nonetheless at a virtual standstill during October. The immediate problem was finally solved when Diem was killed during the coup of 1–2 November.

During the crisis South Vietnam armed forces strength fell by approximately 3,000 spaces, down to a total of 216,000 troops, while increases of about 11,500 men were made in the Civil Guard and Self-Defense Corps and 3,000 for the Civilian Irregular Defense Group. Civil Guard strength rose to 85,900, the Self-Defense Corps remained around 100,000, and the Civilian Irregular Defense Group totaled 18,000 by the end of the year. The "home militia" character of the gaining units had always made them popular in times of stress. But these statistics obscured high desertion rates and constant personnel turnover. At the same time, the activation

LONELY OUTPOST OF SELF-DEFENSE CORPS

of new combat units within the regular Army and the territorial forces continued unabated. The South Vietnam Army, comprising the bulk of the regular forces with 192,000 men, was now organized into 4 corps, 9 divisions, 1 airborne brigade, 1 Special Forces group, 3 separate regiments, 1 territorial regiment, 86 Ranger companies, and 19 separate battalions and associated support units. American military strength also continued to increase and by the end of 1963 reached a new high of 16,263. Of this number 3,150 were assigned to Military Assistance Advisory Group, Vietnam, and 1,451 of these were designated advisory personnel.

The civil unrest and political instability that gripped the Republic of Vietnam from 1963 to 1965 had disastrous effects on the armed forces whose morale dropped to a new low by mid-1964. Two successive coups created numerous changes in the command structure and seriously impaired the administrative and military efficiency of the Army. Short tenures prevented commanders from gaining the full support of their troops, and the confusion was further aggravated by junior officers who openly expressed dissatisfaction and spread discontent among the rank and file. In this atmosphere there was little incentive for conducting normal operations, and the war effort ground to a halt. By the end of 1964 the enemy had clearly seized the initiative, North Vietnamese Army units had been committed, and larger Viet Cong units were maneuvering around the capital area. Once again the survival of the government of South Vietnam was in doubt.

American response to the deteriorating situation was marked by great urgency. The advisory effort was tightened by several major organizational changes in 1964. On 27 January, Lieutenant General William C. Westmoreland was appointed as the first Deputy Commander, U.S. Military Assistance Command, Vietnam, with his principal concern being the advisory structure and all forms of support to the South Vietnamese armed forces. On 15 May, Military Assistance Advisory Group, Vietnam, was combined with Military Assistance Command, Vietnam, and the military support organization was finally united with the advisory effort. This consolidation ended duplication of effort, economized on personnel, and simplified co-ordination. On 20 June General William C. Westmoreland became Commander, U.S. Military Assistance Command, Vietnam.

By the time of the Secretary of Defense conference in June 1964, it was apparent that a further buildup of U.S. strength was necessary to prevent more serious battlefield reverses. One outcome of the conference was the decision to extend the U.S. advisory effort down to district level in the seven key provinces surrounding Saigon. This extension would shore up South Vietnam's emergency *Hop Tac program,* a concentrated effort to ensure the security of the critical capital area. To support this and other programs, by mid-July a total of 4,200 more U.S. troops were moving to Vietnam. With every increase in the advisory effort, additional logistical and administrative support systems were required, as well as more helicopters to support the South Vietnamese Army and U.S. agencies.

Another significant decision was the assignment of the 5th Special Forces Group (Airborne) to Vietnam on a permanent basis. As the 1,300 men of this unit began to arrive by the end of the year, along with the 4,200 additional troops that had been requested in July, U.S. strength rose to a total of 23,310.

It was also now apparent that the South Vietnamese armed forces levels were still too low to satisfy South Vietnam's security needs without sacrificing their own training and reorganization requirements. To remedy this shortage a joint U.S.–South Vietnamese study was made to determine the appropriate force structure required to support the war effort. The study developed two proposals: the first provided for an increase of 30,309 men in the regular forces, 35,387 in the Regional Forces, and 10,815 in the Popular Forces. These forces would support only the *Hop Tac* program and arrest Viet Cong operations in a number of other high-priority areas. The second proposal outlined an increase of 47,556 in regular forces and the same increase in the Regional and Popular Forces. This increased force was considered adequate for substantial over-all progress in pacification but would take considerable time to recruit, train, and equip. On 23 January 1965 the first alternative, with some modification, was formally approved for MAP support. The new force levels were fixed at 275,058 for regular forces, 137,187 for Regional Forces, and 185,000 for Popular Forces. Whether this financial support could be translated into a more effective army was another question.

Training of the South Vietnamese Army, 1960–1964

Poor training or its complete absence was a continual handicap for all South Vietnam armed forces units. Many units had been formed and filled out with hastily drafted personnel with no formal training who were expected to learn by doing. High desertion rates also kept unit personnel in a constant state of flux and made unit retraining a pressing need. After 1960, owing to increasing force levels, the creation of many new units, and the need to acquire counterinsurgency capabilities, training activities took on added emphasis.

Military Assistance Command, Vietnam, assisted the government of Vietnam by drawing up proposed training programs, suggesting specific programs of instruction, providing on-the-spot advice at training centers, and deploying mobile training teams to assist in specific areas such as intelligence, psychological warfare, communications, civil affairs, logistics, and medical training.

By June 1960 Military Assistance Advisory Group, Vietnam, instituted a full-scale counterinsurgency training program within the Vietnamese Army, and by November three Special Forces operational detachments were training 1,200 selected military leaders of the Vietnamese Army in tactics and techniques of counterinsurgency operations. Most of these early efforts were centered around the training given to the newly formed Ranger units by U.S. Special Forces personnel. In 1961 a centralized Ranger Training Center was established at Duc My complete with jungle, swamp, and mountain schools, and there by February 1962 the last of the twenty-one newly activated Ranger companies completed their training. Meanwhile, U.S. Army training teams had been conducting on-site training courses for Ranger companies in the field. In November 1961 these courses had been extended from three to five weeks, and by February 1962 twenty-seven companies had received this instruction and the remainder would finish by the end of the year. At Duc My, individual replacements for Ranger units continued to be trained and the school became a center for counterinsurgency operations.

Counterinsurgency training for regular Vietnamese Army units received less direct emphasis. The newly activated South Vietnamese Army 9th Infantry Division began a 22-week training program in March 1961, and in July the 25th Infantry Division was activated and undertook a similar course. Later, in each of the three corps tactical zones, Military Assistance Advisory Group established a regimental training center staffed with U.S. advisers and Vietnamese cadres. Vietnamese Army infantry regiments were to be rotated through the centers for a seventeen-week refresher course. Training proceeded satisfactorily through 1962 but, as noted above, began to reflect the political and military turbulence at the end of 1963.

During 1964 recruit training was drastically changed. At the beginning of the year plans called for the training of 30,000 recruits at the Quang Trung Training Center, and in January the advisory group recommended that the programs of instruction for basic combat training and advanced individual training be revised to eliminate duplication and correspond more closely to counterinsurgency requirements. This extensive revision was accomplished by March for all arms and services. But by now the military situation was seriously deteriorating and morale was low.

In May the Vietnam government decision to bring The Vietnam Army strength up to authorized force levels resulted in a requirement to train some 40,000 recruits during the remaining seven months of the year. In light of this substantial training increase, Military Assistance Command (Military Assistance Advisory Group was combined with Military Assistance Command on 15 May 1964) recommended that recruit training be expanded from Quang Trung to four other national training centers and to the Ranger Training Center at Duc My. To allow for the increased capacity at the four national training centers, an emergency construction program was immediately initiated for housing, ranges, and other facilities. In addition, Military Assistance Command reluctantly approved a reduction of the recruit training program from twelve to nine weeks. Without the reduction, it would have been impossible to accommodate the large number of recruits unless combat divisions were required to conduct part of the training. The reduced nine-week program began on 1 June and continued for the remainder of 1964. By then over 45,000 recruits had been trained or were in training at these centers. Experience in the latter part of 1964 showed that initial misgivings over the inadequacy of the nine-week program were well founded, and on MACV's recommendation the twelve-week program was readopted on 1 January 1965.

Unit training continued to pose serious problems. In 1963 and 1964 the increased level of enemy activity made it almost impossible to regroup entire combat units for training despite the increased force levels. Only the Ranger battalions were able to complete their initial training and thereafter maintain a continuous retraining program using a six-week cycle. For the Vietnam Army infantry, initial plans called for two battalions from each corps to be in training at all times. In January 1964, eight battalions were in unit training for a four-week cycle which was extended to five weeks in April. However, by May the number of battalions undergoing training had dropped from eight to four because of operational requirements, and by September each corps headquarters was finding it difficult to release even a single battalion for formal training.

Field advisers continued to report that the low state of training was one of the major causes of the low level of combat effectiveness. In spite of this report, formal infantry battalion training continued to slide during the year until, by December 1964, there was only one battalion in training at a national training center. Although 25 infantry battalions had been trained and 8 battalions retrained during the year, there still remained 15 that had not received any formal unit training.

Refresher training of artillery and armored cavalry units continued throughout 1964. In July an intensive retraining program for divisional 4.2-inch mortar battalions being converted to 105-mm. howitzer battalions began and was completed in January 1965. Transition training of armored reconnaissance troops receiving the new M113 armored personnel carriers, begun in April, was completed by November.

During the year Military Assistance Command also proposed new programs of instruction for replacement training, operational readiness training, leadership training, and basic unit training. Although a revised basic unit program of instruction (seven weeks) was adopted and the revised program of instruction for leaders (seven weeks for squadron leaders and ten weeks for platoon leaders) was under consideration, no action was taken on the proposals for replacement or operational readiness programs of instruction.

Combat readiness programs met with even less success. Continued MACV recommendations to establish an effective system of combat readiness training finally resulted in the publication of an implementing directive in September 1964, but this directive had little impact and at the end of the year little effective training was being accomplished outside of schools and training centers.

Air Support

Between 1960 and 1964 greatly increased air support was made available to the South Vietnam Army and should have enabled them to retain the initiative. However, lack of training in airmobile operations proved a severe handicap. The unfamiliarity of both Vietnamese commanders and their MAAGV advisers with the capabilities and limitations of helicopters hindered the effectiveness of early helicopter operations. Too often incomplete premission briefings led to poor co-ordination of air-to-air and air-to-ground operations while all American and Vietnamese aircraft engaged in a mission were airborne. The inability to communicate with supporting Vietnamese fighter aircraft, because of the language barrier and because of differences in communications equipment, also hampered early operations. The incompatibility of U.S. Army UHF helicopter radios and Vietnamese fighter aircraft VHF equipment necessitated the use of a control aircraft to relay messages between the two elements in the air. This method was too cumbersome to support the fast-moving tactical situations and often messages were not retransmitted accurately. The language barrier was still a serious problem even after compatible equipment was installed in late 1962, especially during an operation, when last-minute changes or adjustment became necessary. English-speaking Vietnamese pilots helped to overcome this barrier, but such skills were scarce.

The Vietnamese armed forces unfamiliarity with heliborne operations and other refinements of modern warfare taxed the already overstrained personnel situation of the helicopter companies and served to limit their operational capability. U.S. Army flight personnel found it necessary to devote valuable time to orienting and training Vietnamese fliers in such basic activities as loading, off-loading, and safety procedures while in flight. Vietnamese commanders had to be instructed on the need of separating troops into single aircraft loads to facilitate loading, and on the need of ordering troops to board aircraft with weapons on "safe."

Reluctance to off-load from a hovering helicopter and the tendency to bunch up in the immediate landing zone instead of dispersing rapidly to secure an area often delayed the landing of following helicopters and exposed aircraft and personnel to hostile fire. U.S. helicopter personnel presumed that Vietnamese reluctance to off-load from a hovering aircraft was the result of depth perception errors which made the helicopter appear to be much higher off the ground than it actually was; again, lack of training was the real villain.

The South Vietnam Army provided artillery and mortar support fire in many helicopter operations, but its inaccuracy and undependability made it necessary to halt all fire within a ten-kilometer radius of the landing zone; this ban eliminated valuable close fire support to ground troops and helicopters at the time when they needed it most. Craters created by artillery fire presented hazards to heliborne operations, and flight paths into landing zones sometimes had to be altered because of the location of Vietnamese gun target lines. On one occasion in early 1963 the South Vietnam Army began its artillery preparation of the landing areas too far in advance of the aerial deployment and compromised the element of surprise. The fire was also employed in such a manner as to cause the Viet Cong to move in toward the landing area instead of away from it.

Vietnamese fighter escort aircraft, when they used napalm to clear landing zones, often made the strikes just before the helicopters arrived; the resulting fire and smoke constituted a serious hazard to the helicopters. U.S. helicopters pilots also voiced dissatisfaction with the performance of Vietnamese fighter escort for various other reasons: speed differences between the slow helicopters and fast fighters; withdrawals of fighter aircraft to an altitude of 1,000 feet over the landing or pickup zone, depriving the helicopters of valuable protection at a time when they were most vulnerable to, and most frequently subjected to, hostile fire; and fighter aircraft often abandoning helicopters to assist in ground operations. During the third quarter of calendar year 1962, air support flown by Vietnamese pilots was described by the U.S. helicopter personnel as inadequate, inaccurate, un-co-ordinated, and useless.

To remedy the situation, the Air Force component command of U.S. Military Assistance Command, Vietnam, in late December 1962, established standard tactics and procedures to be used by fighter aircraft when escorting helicopter formations. Supposedly designed to accommodate the flight tactics used by the helicopters in performing their various missions, the regulations, nevertheless, still stipulated that ". . . standard strafing, rocket, napalm or bomb attacks will be made immediately prior to helicopter landings . . ." and that ". . . fighters will orbit the landing zone at an approximately 1,000 feet absolute altitude searching and available to attack on call . . . ." A more successful endeavor was the Air-Ground Operations Mobile Training Team, a joint U.S.–Vietnamese team, which toured schools, training centers, and units during 1964 to familiarize ground troops and especially commanders with air operations.

Other obstacles stemming from training deficiencies were common. Vietnamese confusion in converting weight estimates from the metric system to the avoirdupois weight system sometimes resulted in the overloading of helicopters. Stringent Vietnamese restrictions on night flying and the refusal of local air units to fly night missions to illuminate landing zone areas also restricted the night operational capability of the helicopter units. To overcome this difficulty, some helicopter units trained their own crews to drop flares and diverted valuable aircraft needed elsewhere for such tasks.

Poor intelligence was another handicap. Often Vietnamese combat troops took two to three hours to react to an enemy raid that required quick action. This lessened the effectiveness of airmobile operations in mounting "fire-brigade" type missions, for which U.S. Army helicopter units themselves had a reaction time of only one hour. At the end of 1962 plans were underway for developing small alert force operations to cut the time lapse between "alert announcement" and " on target" to less than an hour.

Role of the U.S. Army Special Forces

Before September 1962 U.S. Army Special Forces personnel served in South Vietnam on a temporary duty basis with MAAGV mobile training teams to provide training for the Vietnamese Army and assist in the CIDG Program. As early as 1957 a team from the 14th Special Forces Operations Detachment on Okinawa trained fifty-eight South Vietnam Army troops at the Commando Training Center at Nha Trang. These Vietnamese troops later became the instructors and cadres for the first Vietnamese Special Forces units. In mid-1960, when the Vietnamese Army established three Ranger training centers at Da Nang, Nha Trang, and Song Mao to train sixty Ranger companies, U.S. Continental Army Command

(USCONARC) sent thirty individuals from the 7th Special Forces Group to South Vietnam on TDY to set up the training course. A nine-man movile training team (four from the 1st Special Forces Group on Okinawa and five from the 25th Infantry Division in Hawaii) replaced the earlier team in 1961. Personnel from the new mobile training team went to Da Nang and Nha Trang to supervise Ranger cadre training and the remainder went to Song Mao to support preparations for the Civil Guard training program. A twelve-man mobile training team from the 1st Special Forces Group in turn replaced the nine-man team on 1 June 1961 and afterwards the 1st Group provided other mobile training teams to South Vietnam to train Vietnamese Army troops. In January 1962 the chief of Military Assistance Advisory Group, Vietnam, requested an augmentation of sixty-eight Special Forces men (twelve officers and fifty-six enlisted men) to advise and assist the Vietnamese Special Forces, the Vietnamese border patrol, and the Montagnard units. He proposed to organize the Special Forces augmentation into one modified B (command and control) and four A (operational) detachments. The Department of Defense rejected the proposal at first, owing to increased Special Forces commitments in other areas of the world, but finally in September approved the principle of placing Special Forces units in South Vietnam on a permanent change of station, or permanent status.

After the arrival in Vietnam of the advance Special Forces team and its designation as Headquarters, U.S. Army Special Forces (Provisional), Vietnam, in September 1962, the headquarters remained at Saigon, sharing administrative tasks with CAS Saigon until 12 February 1963. The new headquarters then moved to Nha Trang, a more central location from which to control and logistically support the CIDG Program.

Special Forces strength in Vietnam remained fairly constant throughout 1963, starting at 625 in January and reaching 674 by the end of June (of which 646 were trained Special Forces personnel). The June totals included 98 on permanent change of station at the headquarters, 24 in TDY C detachment at the headquarters, 524 on TDY in B and A detachments, and 28 with other TDY teams—a Civil Affairs Mobile Training Team and three U.S. Army Engineer Control and Advisory teams. In December two U.S. Navy Special Technical Advisory teams of one officer and thirteen men each began working with the Special Forces in the CIDG Program. And in the following year, as related above, the entire 5th Special Forces Group arrived in Vietnam. By this time most of their training activities centered around the Civilian Irregular Defense Group.

The Civilian Irregular Defense Group Program

CAS Saigon originally began the CIDG Program in December 1961 as a covert operation to win over and train Montagnards and other isolated ethnic minority groups into an anti-Viet Cong irregular, paramilitary force. The Civilian Irregular Defense Group had among other missions that of collecting intelligence in the highlands of central South Vietnam and in Laos, where tribal affiliations were used extensively to further clandestine activities. The program also had a civic action aspect, and CAS provided medical treatment, medicines, seeds, clothing, and other social welfare goods to win over the ethnic groups. After the U.S. Army asumed control over the overt activities of the CIDG Program, the medical phase of civic action evolved into the Special Forces Village Defense Medical Program.

The CIDG Program rapidly grew to include overt activities and embraced other paramilitary groups such as the republican youth, Catholic youth, hamlet militia, strike forces, mountain commandos, trailwatchers, fighting fathers, and force populaire. Most of these organizations served mainly to relieve the South Vietnam armed forces, the Civil Guard, and the Self-Defense Corps troops from static defense missions. Therefore, the nature of their activities were in the main defensive; but such groups as the strike forces, mountain commandos, and trailwatchers aggressively sought out the Viet Cong. The strike forces and mountain commandos operated against existing enemy units, while the trailwatchers tried to prevent infiltration into South Vietnam. When infiltrating forces were too large for a trailwatcher group to handle, it reported the presence of the enemy to the nearest Vietnamese Army corps headquarters.

The U.S. Army Special Forces overtly entered into the CIDG Program on 1 February 1962 when sixteen Special Forces troops began assisting CAS Saigon in training selected Vietnamese in special warfare activities. By the end of April 1962, seventy-five Special Forces men were providing CAS with assistance in training, advising, and supporting the various activities of the program.

By April 1962 it was becoming evident that the expanding CIDG Program was straining the capabilities of CAS Saigon, and the commander of Military Assistance Command in Vietnam recommended that direct U.S. military support be made available. In mid-July the Secretary of Defense agreed and launched Operation SWITCHBACK, the code name for MACV's assumption of the covert aspect of the CIDG Program. During the transitional period CAS Saigon continued supporting the entire program; after the

CIDG Unit Training

takeover CAS was responsible for only the covert aspects of the effort, and the Army continued to provide CAS with Special Forces type training assistance when requested. Military Assistance Command had operational control over the overt aspects of the program throughout the transitional period. After 1 July 1963 the bulk of the Special Forces effort together with the CIDG Program fell under complete MACV control. By October 1963 this group amounted to 16,084 strike force members, 40,765 hamlet militiamen, 4,912 mountain scouts, and 3,256 border surveillance personnel.

Territorial Forces: Civil Guard and Self-Defense Corps

Between 1960 and 1964 the territorial forces received more training but were still stepchildren of the growing South Vietnam armed forces family. One basic problem was organizational. While these units were operationally controlled by province and district officials, training was usually an Army responsibility. Nevertheless, beginning in 1960 much effort was expended on strengthening the operational capability of the Civil Guard and the Self-Defense

Corps by improving their training and supplying them with weapons and communications equipment. To speed up Civil Guard training new unit training centers were opened, and the training cycle was reduced from twenty-four to twelve weeks. In addition, joint MAAGV–Civil Guard training teams were formed to instruct both Civil Guard and Self-Defense Corps units at their operational bases. The Self-Defense Corps, now supported by MAP funds, was reorganized into squads and platoons and underwent intensified training. Training centers were established in twenty-six provinces where a six-week program of instruction was offered. MAAGV's goal was to have all Self-Defense Corps units completely equipped and trained by the end of 1962.

Before 1964 no established recruit training program for the Regional Forces (formerly the Civil Guard) had existed. Many units were little more than armed bands of young men; others were private armies and gangs "federalized" into the service of the government of Vietnam. Military Assistance Command recommended a plan to train 4,000 recruits in 1964 but, although the plan was approved and scheduled to begin in April, training fell short because of recruiting difficulties. In June the Regional Forces began conscripting personnel in order to reach a goal of 14,000 recruits; however, owing to the priority given to the Vietnam Army, few recruits were obtained and at the end of the year only about 2,000 had received training while about 700 were undergoing training. The recruit training program of instruction of nine weeks was the same as that used in the Vietnamese Army training centers. This approach at least allowed the Regional Forces training centers to train Vietnamese Army recruits when their own quotas fell short.

Because of force structure increases and other demands, Regional Forces unit training also expanded in 1964. By May the number of Regional Forces companies had risen from 473 to 523 and in November plans were made to increase this total to 640. Objectives for calendar year 1964 included unit training for all new Regional Forces companies and refresher training for approximately 60 percent of the existing units. By the end of the year, 533 Regional Forces companies had been organized, of which 494 were trained, 20 were training, and 19 remained to be trained. Of the 533 companies, 196 had completed the four-week refresher course and seven were in refresher training.

With the lowest recruiting priority, the Popular Forces (formerly the Self-Defense Corps) suffered grave deficiencies in all aspects of training. Popular Forces strength initially fell far behind programed force levels until July 1964, and leadership training quotas were never filled during the entire year. Training had been programed for the year based on an authorized force structure of 110,000. But serious training lags developed early in the year owing to the late publication of the 1964 program, difficulties in recruiting, and the reluctance of province chiefs to relinquish their units to training centers because of local security conditions. Thus, despite much emphasis by Military Assistance Command, both units and leadership training continued to trail as much as 60 percent behind programed levels. On October 1964 Military Assistance Command proposed the consolidation of Popular Forces training centers to improve facilities and the conduct of training and reduce cost of manpower and matériel without reducing the over-all training base capacity. In addition, a proposal was made to turn over the training responsibility of the Regional and Popular Forces from the Vietnamese Training Command to the national Regional and Popular Forces headquarters in order to ensure unity of effort. However, as yet there was no agreement as to which agency should be responsible.

Civil Affairs

In the course of a staff visit to South Vietnam in early 1960 to determine the assistance needed in civil affairs activities, a member of the U.S. Army, Pacific, G–5 section determined that Military Assistance Advisory Group, Vietnam, could profitably employ a civil affairs mobile training team to develop a civil affairs capability within the South Vietnam armed forces. In May 1960 the chief of the advisory group requested the team, and two officers from the Civil Affairs School at Fort Gordon, Georgia, arrived in July for a ninety-day tour of duty. The officers instructed MAAGV and ARVN personnel in civil affairs and civic action and advised and assisted the MAAGV chief on all aspects of civil affairs operations and activities.

For various reasons, including the unfavorable attitude of the South Vietnamese and the fact that the advisory group had no civil affairs officer, the succeeding year saw no tangible results develop from the team's visit. The next significant step came in May 1961 when the MAAGV chief requested a civil affairs mobile training team to conduct a survey, and to assist the advisory group and the Vietnamese Army in developing and implementing civic action projects and programs in accordance with U.S. policies.

Arriving in July, the civil affairs mobile training team was composed of two officers (one a public administrator and the other a public health officer) and one enlisted administrative assistant;

it worked in Vietnam from July to December 1961 and developed a comprehensive civic action program for consideration by the MAAGV chief and the South Vietnamese. The mobile training team also outlined a civil affairs organization needed to help build security in areas liberated from Viet Cong control and recommended actions the South Vietnamese armed forces could take to improve economic, social, and political development of the people. The program, prepared by the team in directive form, was submitted through the MAAGV Chief to the government of South Vietnam. The proposed directive provided instruction concerning responsibilities; guidance, as well as examples, for civic action projects; needs of the population; and training, supply, and necessary administration. Although the South Vietnam government did not initiate the program immediately, it used the plan as the basis for its civic action program.

Meanwhile, in August 1961, the MAAGV chief reported that the Vietnamese Army had conducted two otherwise successful division-size operations which typically devoted inadequate attention to civil-military co-ordination. He reported that "plans for followup pacification of area made by government delegate for area not adequately coordinated and apparently include little or no integration of military and civil operations. Rather, civil plans were separate and not intended to be implemented until operation was completed." The report, plus the results of the mobile training team's survey, indicated a pressing need to improve civic action measures of the South Vietnam armed forces if counterinsurgency operations were to succeed.

During the same period and at the MAAGV Chief's request, the Department of the Army permitted the South Vietnam government to send seventy-five officers to the Civil Affairs School at Fort Gordon, Georgia. From a Vietnamese point of view, the training received was not completely satisfactory because of the difference in staff organization and the school's emphasis on large-scale, military government. At the same time, at the advisory group's instigation, the Vietnam armed forces instituted for military province and district chiefs an eighteen-week civil affairs course of instruction which proved more closely attuned to South Vietnam's immediate needs.

Before the mobile training team departed in December 1961, it helped organize two experimental South Vietnam Army civil affairs companies, made a list of projects to be accomplished by the Vietnam armed forces, and briefed top U.S. and South Vietnamese military and civilian leaders on the importance and need for civic action. As a result of the mobile training teams work, planning began that visualized the use of the Self-Defense Corps in the dual role of village defense and civic action. Military Assistance Advisory Group continued co-ordination with the U.S. Operation Mission on military civic action planning conducted through the offices of the Country Team's Psychological Warfare Subcommittee. By December 1961 the MAAGV chief added to his staff a civil affairs officer who served as Chief, Civil Affairs and Psychological Warfare Branch, Organization and Training Division. This branch was responsible for all civil affairs and psychological warfare advisory duties.

In August 1962, at the request of the Commander, Military Assistance Command, Vietnam, the 97th Civil Affairs Group provided a five-man mobile training team for five weeks to prepare a program of instruction for a civil affairs course at the South Vietnam Army Psychological Warfare School, and also to prepare a training program for use by the Vietnamese civil affairs companies. The mobile training team improved the Vietnamese civil affairs course and launched the training program for the newly activated companies. Concurrent with drawing up plans for assignment of this team, U.S. advisers convinced the South Vietnamese director of Psychological Warfare of the need for more civil affairs units, and in September 1962 the South Vietnam Army directed the activation of three civil affairs companies, one for employment in each of the three corps areas. Later in 1962, with the formation of the IV South Vietnam Army Corps, a fourth Vietnamese Army civil affairs company was authorized. The Vietnam Army officially activated the first three companies on 14 December 1962.

On 11 October 1962 the MAAGV chief requested four civil affairs mobile training teams (each to consist of nine officers and four enlisted men) for 180 days TDY to provide training, advice, and assistance to South Vietnamese personnel in conducting programs for "clearing and holding provinces from Viet Cong forces." Three of the teams arrived on 15 December 1962 and the fourth on 5 January 1963. Each South Vietnam Army corps received one team in order to provide specialized assistance to the Strategic Hamlet Program, advise Vietnamese civil affairs teams, assist in the medical civic action program, and to assist Operations Mission field representatives. In June the four mobile training teams were replaced by a 21-man team attached to the U.S. Army Special Forces (Provisional), Vietnam, for 180 days' TDY to support the CIDG Program. In addition to these units there were also a Medical Civil Action Group and several Engineer Control and

Advisory detachments active in Vietnam and supporting specific South Vietnam programs.

In May 1963 the South Vietnam Army recalled their four civil affairs companies for re-equipping, reorganizing, and retraining. Their initial experiences were evaluated and their concept of operation revised. By early July 1963 the units had completed retraining and redeployed to the field with forty D teams; each province received one team and the infantry divisions absorbed the remainder. These teams had mixed success, but in general were not strong enough to push the more important civil affairs projects, such as the Strategic Hamlet Program, that the South Vietnam government was trying to complete. Needless to say, the declining fortunes of South Vietnam in 1964 also adversely affected both the capabilities and potential of these units.

At the end of 1964 it appeared that Military Assistance Command, Vietnam, had been too optimistic regarding the various training programs. Field reports continued to point out that poor training and a shortage of good junior leaders were still the main factors behind South Vietnam armed forces marginal combat effectiveness. Military Assistance Command, Vietnam, tended to become impatient when training programs were delayed and statistical quotas not met. Finally the buildup of Viet Cong strength and activity put too great a strain on the limited South Vietnam armed forces resources to permit unit rotation through the training centers. Pacification progress and troop retraining were simply incompatible with existing force levels. One problem fed upon another, and as the situation deteriorated recruiting became more difficult and desertions more common. Major political and military decisions would have to be made if the training situation was to improve.

CHAPTER III

The Buildup Years, 1965–1967

Background

The situation at the beginning of 1965 was critical. By taking advantage of the civil unrest and political instability that had prevailed since mid-1963, the enemy had grown stronger and tightened his hold on the countryside. Estimates of enemy strength had risen from a total of 30,000 in November 1963 to 212,000 by July 1965. The Viet Cong launched their first division-size attack against the village of Binh Gia close to Saigon where they destroyed two South Vietnam Army battalions and remained on the battlefield for four days instead of following their usual hit-and-run tactics. North Vietnamese units and reinforcements had now joined the battle and were arriving at a rate of nearly 1,000 men per month. Both the North Vietnam Army and the Viet Cong were now armed with modern weapons such as the AK47 assault rifle, giving them a firepower advantage over the South Vietnam Army which was still fighting with American weapons of World War II vintage. Enemy strategy was evidently based on the assumption that the United States would not increase its involvement and that, weak as it was, the government of South Vietnam would collapse from its own weight if pushed hard enough.

After the death of President Diem in November 1963, South Vietnam had been controlled by a number of coalition governments. Each proved incapable of providing centralized direction to the war effort, and the pacification program ground to a halt. The majority of rural areas still remained under Viet Cong control or were "contested" in the enemy's favor. The involvement of military officials in the political upheaval, the consequent widespread reassignment and adjustments within the military command and staff structure, and the setbacks in offensive operations, all brought armed forces morale and effectiveness to a new low. The internal turmoil and collapse of the government also severely hampered mobilization and recruiting efforts. Almost all combat units were below authorized strength and desertion rates continued to soar. Some paramilitary units simply disbanded and melted away; the better South Vietnam Army units were spending most of their energies reacting to enemy initiatives. It was apparent that the South Vietnam government could not prevent the enemy from taking over the country.

Consideration of and planning for the introduction of U.S. combat forces into South Vietnam began in late 1964. These forces were to be used primarily to defend and secure U.S. installations and activities. Further planning received impetus on 7 February 1965, when the Viet Cong attacked the MACV Advisor Compound and the Camp Holloway airfield at Pleiku. American forces suffered 136 casualties and twenty-two aircraft were damaged or destroyed. Three days later, Viet Cong terrorists destroyed the enlisted billets in Qui Nhon causing forty-four more American losses. These events demanded a strong response.

Obviously the war was entering a new phase for the United States. In spite of its ever-increasing aid and buildup of advisory and operational support personnel, it had not been able to reverse the deteriorating military situation. Only new and decisive action on its part could prevent the collapse of the government of South Vietnam.

Military Assistance Command Advisory Expansion

In early 1965 the United States met the challenge with the decision to introduce U.S. combat forces into South Vietnam. The arrival of U.S. Marine units at Da Nang in March 1965 was followed by a massive buildup of U.S. forces over the next three years. A peak strength of more than 543,000 was reached in May 1969. While U.S. combat forces undoubtedly prevented the military defeat of the South Vietnam government, American assumption of the major combat role has been the subject of much controversy. Critics have charged that the United States took the war away from the Vietnamese and made participation in the struggle meaningless for them. "Why fight when the Americans will fight our battles for us?" many argued. Americans have been accused of letting impatience blur their long-range vision for developing the Vietnamese military forces and of being too prone to do the job themselves. But, again, the claim must be taken into account that without U.S. combat intervention, the South Vietnam armed forces would have ceased to exist.

General Westmoreland divided the U.S. effort in South Vietnam into two parts: first, the tactical effort to destroy the Viet Cong and North Vietnam Army main force units and, second, the effort to help South Vietnam develop a viable government able to exercise effective control throughout the country. The two aims were closely related, with the second calling for a greater emphasis in establishing security in the villages and hamlets, and in the extension of South Vietnam government influence and control. To help accomplish the second objective, sector (province) and subsector (district) advisory teams working with South Vietnam government officials at province and district level had to be strengthened and expanded, and their efforts focused on specific programs and goals.

Concurrent with U.S. combat force buildup, the advisory effort expanded at a rapid pace. Planning for the extension of the advisory program to the subsector level was under U.S. and Vietnamese consideration in late 1963 and early 1964. Military Assistance Command, Vietnam, envisaged that advisory teams would deal primarily with the paramilitary forces (police and pacification cadre) and would supervise most of the unit training, advise the district chief on operations, and assist in operational planning. Experimental teams were planned for deployment in the spring of 1964; if these teams were successful the program was to be expanded later in the year. Planners raised a number of possible objections: some felt that the limited South Vietnamese staff at district level would be overwhelmed by advice and advisers; that Communist propaganda portraying the South Vietnam government as a U.S. puppet would be more effective than American claims, and that the U.S. military-civilian balance in personnel providing pacification advice at the provincial level would be disrupted. In addition, more American personnel in isolated areas would mean greater casualties. Nevertheless, the commander stuck to his decision.

The pilot teams, each consisting of one officer and one noncommissioned officer, began operating in April and May 1964. One team was deployed to each of the thirteen districts in the provinces surrounding Saigon. At first progress was minimal. There was no standard district organization and little similarity between districts. The government of Vietnam was in the process of building up its district staffs and was experiencing its own growing pains. Trained talent was at a premium. For the most part district chiefs were left to develop their own organizations with what limited manpower and talent they could obtain.

Within a month encouraging signs began to emerge. Districts which had been isolated and remote slowly became close members of the provincial family. As communications improved, some districts became active in provincial affairs. Economic and social bonds were made, and military co-ordination was greatly improved. Later, as the teams became firmly established, other advantages began to emerge. Support of all types became available to the district chief who thereby acquired more prestige; at the same time, the U.S. obtained fresh insights into local conditions, activities, requirements, attitudes, and aspirations of the people. The pilot teams did become involved in the U.S. Operations Mission and the U.S. Information Service areas of interest, but without the disruption that had been feared earlier. Advice and assistance was furnished in planning and executing educational, economic, agricultural, youth, and information programs. In fact, the advisory teams in some areas devoted up to 80 percent of their energy to nonmilitary matters. However, usually the amount of time spent was equally divided between military and civil activities.

Basing his action on the gratifying results of the pilot teams, the Secretary of Defense approved plans to expand the program at a conference in Hawaii in June 1964. Planning and preparation for an additional one hundred teams began immediately. Each team would consist of two officers and three enlisted personnel. The title of subsector advisory team was derived from the district's military designation subsector. Prospective team locations were determined from recommendations submitted by senior advisers in each corps area. Terms of reference were developed based on lessons learned by the pilot teams; the teams were instructed to extend the capabilities of the Operations Mission and the Information Service, but only if directed by their local representatives. To better prepare incoming advisory personnel, a two-week Military Assistance Training Advisor course was established in Saigon.

By 1965 the planning and preparations had paid dividends, and the deployment of the additional teams was practically complete. Most of the advantages claimed by the pilot teams were verified and many of those who had voiced strong opinion against the program were won over. The new teams met and overcame the same basic problems that the original thirteen had encountered. They enthusiastically assumed broad and unfamiliar responsibilities with very little specific guidance. Guidance was purposely general and, as was made abundantly clear, variety was the only consistency at subsector level. As the sole U.S. representation below provincial level, the team was the sole executor of the U.S. effort in the South Vietnamese countryside.

By the end of the year many new districts were under consideration for assignment of advisory teams, and with some locations slated to receive U.S. Army Special Forces A detachments. Under study were ways to determine the best means of augmenting team capabilities (operations, training, security, and so forth) and of supporting teams with certain hard skills (intelligence, engineer, medical, and other skills). Missions and duties were also under revision to better suit the changing situation.

Also by the end of the year, 169 subsector advisory teams had deployed (133 MACV and 36 Special Forces men), with a total strength of about 1,100. Advisory teams were also assigned to all forty-three sectors (38 MACV and 5 Special Forces men). Over-all field advisory strength rose from 4,741 to 5,377 in 1965. It should be noted that these individuals were almost all experienced officers and noncommissioned officers, and thus represented a commitment not reflected in the bare statistical data.

The program continued to expand over the next several years. Although the results achieved were encouraging, continued evaluation and improvements were made. During the same period, the U.S. combat buildup generated an urgent demand for resources, talent, and command attention. Planners had to take care to ensure that the advisory teams were not slighted. The program, although relatively small, had proved to have a widespread and important influence on the war, with the effectiveness of the program depending on quality rather than quantity. A major study was initiated in June 1966 to evaluate and determine ways to improve the effectiveness of the sector and subsector advisory teams. In assessing the program planners analyzed the team composition, team-member training, and the command emphasis necessary to improve the program. The following recommendations of the study were approved by General Westmoreland on 1 July.

1. The greatest degree of tailoring of the subsector team organization to fit conditions should be encouraged, and the composition of all subsector teams should be evaluated in light of additional skills available; the composition should be altered where necessary to suit the situation of each district (psychological operations advisers, civil affairs advisers, engineer advisers, and so forth).

2. Special attention should be directed to the selection and preparatory training of officers designated as subsector advisers, including a twelve-week language course and a six-week civil affairs adviser course. Military Assistance Command recommended that preparatory training courses for subsector advisers be consolidated at one location in continental United States to relieve the necessity for extended temporary duty before the assignment of future advisers to South Vietnam.

3. Command emphasis is needed to make the advisory effort a priority program and ensure that officers assigned as subsector advisers not be used to fill other spaces in the command, and that

officers serving as subsector advisers serve their full tour in that capacity.

4. Exact requirements for helicopter support throughout the country for sector and subsector advisers should be determined, and a special priority allocation of helicopter resources should be made to meet those requirements.

By late 1966, reassignment of sector and subsector advisory personnel was minimal and authorized only for compelling reasons. General Westmoreland was concerned with obtaining stability of personnel and wanted every effort made to ensure that these positions had at least the minimum degree of continuity. In addition, steps were taken to extend selected advisers of unique experience or qualifications up to one year beyond the normal tour length. Extensions were to be both voluntary and involuntary, but in practice only those willing to have their tours extended were nominated.

In 1967, with new adviser requirements still being generated, analysts undertook a major study to examine the current advisory effort and review the existing strength authorizations and requirements that had been identified in the fiscal year 1968 South Vietnam armed forces structure. Brigadier General Edward M. Flanagan, Jr., then Training Directorate chief of Military Assistance Command in Vietnam, supervised the study; his objective was to develop the framework on which an improved advisory program could be constructed using the existing organization as a point of departure. Further, the study was to determine if the existing efforts were being properly applied and to recommend any reorientation deemed appropriate. The study recommendations called for a deletion of 1965 advisory spaces from the MACV staff, 940 spaces from the sector advisory chain, and 562 spaces from the tactical advisory chain. The study approved elimination of the spaces from the tactical chain and Military Assistance Command, but the sector chain remained intact.

A second major study undertaken in 1967 was known as Project 640. This study addressed itself to the absence of any central staff agency to co-ordinate and monitor the advisory effort. Past experience had shown that many activities related to the advisory and military assistance effort encompassed many staff areas of interest and that the MACV staff was not appropriately organized to carry out its responsibilities in these matters. The study thus recommended the establishment of a single staff agency to act as the focal point for the advisory effort. By the end of the year, the Office of the Chief of Staff, Military Assistance Command, Military Assistance, (MACMA) had been established under the supervision of Brigadier General Donnelly P. Bolton. The mission of the Military Assistance staff was to supervise, co-ordinate, monitor, and evaluate, in conjunction with appropriate agencies, the joint advisory effort and the Military Assistance Program for the government of Vietnam.

In the same year, 1967, while most of the South Vietnam Army infantry units were being employed in a pacification role, another significant expansion of the advisory effort took place. On a visit to Vietnam in January, the JCS chairman, General Earle G. Wheeler, emphasized the importance of providing physical security to the rural areas and the need "to insure effective transition of this substantial portion of ARVN from search-and-destroy or clear-and-hold operations to local security activities." Wheeler asked, "Is it not essential that these ARVN forces be imbued with the vital importance of their task and be rapidly trained for it, and would it not be wise to assign American officers—as advisors to all ARVN local security detachments of company size and larger?" Subsequent studies indicated the following advantages would accrue by assigning advisers to company-size units:

1. improved combat effectiveness.

2. enhanced unit effectiveness in winning the willing support of the people to the South Vietnam government,

3. improved unit civic action and psychological warfare operations, and

4. expedited completion of the Revolutionary Development (pacification) process.

As a result, additional adviser spaces were requested to provide one additional officer and enlisted man for each battalion conducting independent operations in support of the pacification effort, an effort that U.S. advisers were now indirectly supervising at almost every level.

U.S. Army Special Forces Advisory Programs

On 1 January 1965, U.S. Army Special Forces in Vietnam was organized into four C detachments, five B detachments, forty-four A detachments, and support units. The C detachments were assigned to each corps tactical zone to provide command and control for all U.S. Special Forces elements in the zone, B detachments were intermediate control elements, and A detachments were small teams of twelve to thirteen men which furnished the major portion of the advisory support to the Civilian Irregular Defense Group. Although the number of units was increased as the need arose, their organizational structure remained the same.

In addition to providing advisory support to the CIDG Program and to the sectors and subsectors assigned to them by the MACV commander, the U.S. Army Special Forces provided advisory support to five other endeavors: the Apache Force program, the Mike Force, the Delta Force, the CIDG motivational program, and special intelligence missions.

The Apache Force involved the use of small, highly mobile teams of indigenous personnel. Teams were commanded by a U.S. Special Forces officer, but worked with regular U.S. units and remained under the control of a U.S. unit commander; their mission was to find and fix enemy forces until larger and stronger units could be brought in. They also secured drop zones and landing zones, located enemy lines of communication, and provided intelligence to the U.S. commander. Each team consisted of four pathfinder, reconnaissance, and combat teams to find the enemy, and three CIDG companies to fix him in place. When U.S. forces were committed, the Apache Force came under the operational control of the U.S. commander for the duration of the operation. At the end of the year the program had not been officially implemented, but troops had been recruited in all four corps tactical zones, and CIDG units in the II Corps Tactical Zone were giving this type of support on an informal basis to the 1st Cavalry Division (Airmobile).

Mike Forces were companies of indigenous tribal personnel recruited and held in reserve by each of the C detachments and at the 5th Special Forces Group headquarters at Nha Trang to provide reaction forces in support of CIDG units within the corp tactical zone. These units were not a part of the Civilian Irregular Defense Group but were recruited and paid by U.S. Army Special Forces.

Delta Forces were similar in concept to the Apache units. The force was advised by a U.S. Special Force detachment and consisted of twelve ten-man hunter-killer teams (each composed of two U.S. Special Forces men and eight Vietnamese Special Forces volunteers) and four South Vietnam Army airborne/ranger companies with U.S. Special Forces advisers down to platoon level. This force was supported by four Vietnamese Air Force H-34 helicopters and two Vietnamese C-47 aircraft. The mission of the Delta Force was to infiltrate Viet Cong controlled territory within the borders of South Vietnam and gather intelligence. The airborne/ranger elements permitted the force to exploit lucrative targets immediately; these hunter-killer teams were also used successfully in gathering target intelligence and in assessing B-52 air strikes.

The airborne/ranger companies were also used in support of besieged camps, notably Plei Me in Pleiku Province.

The CIDG motivational program consisted of two groups of approximately fifty Viet Cong defectors recruited, trained, and equipped by U.S. Special Forces; in I and IV Corps Tactical Zones the groups moved into areas under pacification, provided their own security, performed civic action, and furnished motivational indoctrination to the indigenous population. Each team had eight U.S. Special Forces advisors.

Financial Support

Concurrent with the increases in U.S. combat and advisory forces, a massive buildup and training program for the Republic of Vietnam armed forces gradually unfolded. This development was consistent with the U.S. basic commitment—to create a South Vietnamese armed force capable of defending South Vietnam with minimal outside assistance. In this respect limited financial resources was always a pressing problem. It was not until mid-1965 with the appearance of the Ky-Thieu regime that a viable government existed which was able to effectively promulgate economic constraints and enlistment inducements and incentives. Only then could force structure plans be instituted with some assurance that means were available to carry them out.

Under legislation and policies in effect before March 1966, the Republic of Vietnam armed forces was supported through the Military Assistance Program. The program was designed to support friendly nations under peacetime conditions and was restricted by worldwide ceilings established by congressional legislation. During this period, dollar ceilings and equipment requirements recommended through submission of plans and programs to the Office of the Secretary of Defense were not necessarily approved. Programing (and eventual delivery) of equipment during this era was governed by the ceilings authorized and the funds appropriated. The expansion and development of the South Vietnam Army was thus circumscribed by these ceilings, and often only those measures which Military Assistance Command felt were most important were approved. Although these ceilings proved to be sufficiently flexible to enable programing to correct major deficiencies, continual price increases and replacement of equipment lost in combat placed a severe strain on available MAP funds. Other factors limiting the development of the South Vietnam Army under the Military Assistance Program included:

1. restrictions governing offshore (foreign) procurement which

were instituted because of U.S. deficiencies in the international balance of payments;

2. legislative prohibitions on procurement of matériel in anticipation of future appropriations; and the

3. normal practice of supplying older equipment to MAP recipients to purify U.S. stocks.

In March 1966 the support of the Republic of Vietnam armed forces was transferred from the MAP appropriations to the regular defense budget. This measure reduced the strain on the limited MAP funds and allowed U.S. and South Vietnamese military forces to be financed through a common budget. Since then, funding limitations were dependent more on the situation within South Vietnam than in the United States. As a corollary, the government of Vietnam defense budget was limited by U.S. ceilings placed on piaster expenditures. Although these ceilings had no direct limiting effect on improvement of the armed forces, inflationary trends in the economy were a matter of utmost concern when determining the force structure. More and higher paid troops might mean fewer farmers, less taxes, and higher food prices; in this way the piaster ceiling limited expansion. The ceiling also limited U.S. troop spending within South Vietnam.

Manpower Resources

South Vietnamese manpower was another major problem area in the expansion of the Republic of Vietnam armed forces. Difficulties were caused by an ineffective conscription program and a continually high desertion rate. The conscription program dated back to September 1957, but Vietnamese military authorities had never made any real effort to enforce conscription laws, and by the end of 1965 an estimated 232,000 youths had been able to evade military service. More pressure was now placed on the South Vietnam government to correct this problem.

With expansion underway in 1964, Military Assistance Command, Vietnam, undertook a manpower resources survey to determine if sufficient manpower was available in areas of South Vietnam government control to make up the required military forces needed to defeat the insurgency. The survey estimated that about 365,000 men were available and qualified for the regular forces, and that an additional 800,000 men could meet other force requirements. The survey confirmed that the planned force goals were not impossible, and the results were subsequently used as the basis for manpower planning procurement.

Manpower procurement was assisted by the promulgation of

NEW TERRITORIAL RECRUITS

more stringent draft laws during 1964. On 6 April the National Public Service Decree declared that all male Vietnamese citizens from twenty to forty-five years were subject to service in the military and civil defense establishment. Subsequent decrees prescribed draft criteria and lengths of service, and another incorporated the Regional Forces and Popular Forces into the regular force (Republic of Vietnam armed forces) organization. A review of the South Vietnam government laws by a representative of the U.S. National Selective Service concluded that the draft laws were adequate, but better enforcement was urgently needed.

Because of the great concern with manpower problems, the U.S. (Embassy) Mission Personnel and Manpower Committee was established in August 1964. The committee was chaired by the MACV J-1 (Personnel Staff chief) with representation from other U.S. agencies and worked closely with a counterpart South Vietnam committee. The two groups recommended a collective call-up of youths aged twenty to twenty-five followed by a strict enforcement period. The recommendation was approved and in August the government of Vietnam made plans for a preliminary call-up in IV Corps Tactical Zone. The test mobilization pointed out the need for extensive prior planning to include transportation, food, and orientation for the draftees, and these measures were quickly incorporated into a national plan. A Mobilization Directorate was also established in August within the Ministry of Defense to direct the call-up and Military Assistance Command supplied advisory support.

A nationwide call-up was conducted from 20 October to 2 November, and a one-month enforcement phase followed to apprehend and induct draft dodgers. Pre-call-up publicity emphasized that this was the last time youths twenty to twenty-five could voluntarily report and that the "tough" measures to apprehend and punish evaders would follow. Initial results were gratifying as over 11,600 conscripts were inducted into the regular forces. Careful planning, effective publicity, and creditability of the enforcement procedures accounted for the success. Unfortunately, the enforcement phase was less than satisfactory. Its implementation required the execution of detailed procedures by province chiefs and local officials, and this execution was not done in a uniform manner. The failure fully to enforce the initial call-up took the sting out of the program, and subsequent draft calls in late November and early December brought fewer recruits than were anticipated or needed to meet force level goals.

Shortages in draftee quotas made it impossible for the Republic of Vietnam armed forces to meet the proposed force level goals for 1965. General Westmoreland was disappointed and in a letter to Ambassador Maxwell D. Taylor on 16 December 1964 summarized his position:

. . . it is imperative for the GVN to act now to vigorously enforce the call-up; widely publicize the program to discharge personnel who have been involuntarily extended, pointing out the obligation of other citizens to bear arms to make discharges possible; acquire sufficient personnel to offset losses through discharge action and attain authorized force levels; take positive action to prepare for further call-up of personnel by year group to increase the force levels according to current plans.

Although this plea was followed by an announcement that draft dodgers would be rounded up, particularly in the Saigon area, the South Vietnam government had taken no positive action by the end of the year, and it was not until April 1966 that the government issued a new series of decrees to enforce existing draft laws and provide punishment for deserters and their accomplices (these new measures, which are discussed later in the chapter, finally did provide some relief of the turbulent manpower situation).

A second action to increase the manpower of the South Vietnam Army was the initiation of a comprehensive recruiting campaign which included extensive publicity, enlistment bonuses, special

THE BUILDUP YEARS, 1965–1967 59

training for recruiters, and accelerated quotas for unit recruiting. These measures together with the call-up enabled the regular forces to exceed their authorized strength levels by the end of 1964. By mid-1965, however, desertions had eroded all regular force increases and by 1966 the problem was still unsolved.

Because of the urgency of the manpower situation, in June 1966 General Westmoreland directed that a study be made to find a comprehensive solution to the problem. The ensuing study warned that if the current situation continued, the rate of manpower consumption would exhaust primary manpower sources by mid-1968 and secondary military manpower sources by the end of 1969. Government of Vietnam manpower resources still lacked over-all central direction; as a result, there were gross imbalances in the manpower pools which supported the diverse and often conflicting government programs. The single organization charged with manpower planning, the Directorate of Mobilization, was a subordinate agency of the Ministry of Defense and organizationally was not in a position to exert national control over manpower resources. The study concluded that a requirement existed for orderly distribution of available manpower among users, and that a general mobilization would be preferable to a partial mobilization, although the latter would be better than the existing haphazard system. The study recommended the formation of a study group of interested agencies (the Embassy, U.S. Agency for International Development, Military Assistance Command) to analyze available data on manpower and matériel resources and to do the initial planning required. Afterward, a joint U.S.–South Vietnamese commission should be established to analyze the existing governmental structure and determine what additional machinery would be required to accomplish a general mobilization. General Westmoreland agreed with the study's recommendations and on 15 June sent a letter to the U.S. Ambassador supporting its proposals.

General Westmoreland recognized that the demands on military manpower were great and that there was also a heavy and increasing demand for qualified manpower by the private and governmental sectors of South Vietnam. Un-co-ordinated attempts to correct the military problem would have adverse effects on the remaining sectors. While the South Vietnam government had failed to organize itself to meet the heavy calls on its manpower, solutions demanded that a determination be made of total manpower assets and total requirements, and that the two then be balanced. Aware of the serious implications of total mobilization, Westmoreland recommended that a U.S. committee to study mobilization be established under the direction of the Embassy and include USAID and MACV representation. A joint U.S.–South Vietnamese commission would then be set up to integrate the preliminary aspects of the study into a combined program for mobilization which would be appropriate for both governmental and social structures.

When no action was taken on this proposal, General Westmoreland sent in May 1967 a second letter to the U.S. Ambassador on the subject. He again stressed the need for a mobilization plan. As a result, the ambassador established a special manpower advisory mission composed of economic, labor, and management specialists from the United States. This mission, in co-ordination with the Embassy and Military Assistance Command, developed the basic planning necessary for mobilization. Discussions then began with the Vietnamese government, and on 24 October 1967 laws outlining plans for a partial mobilization were decreed. However, there was no implementing legislation and some question existed as to whether the South Vietnam government was strong enough to carry the measures out. At the time, governmental stability was still in critical condition and anything that might threaten that stability or cause the government to be unpopular had to be treated with care.

The Desertion Problem

Desertions continued to be a thorny matter thoughout this period. The encouraging gains in the manpower situation made in late 1964 lasted only briefly owing to the rising number of "unapproved leaves" during 1965. Military Assistance Command undertook several studies to determine the causes for the excessively high desertion rates and noted the following contributing factors:

1. overly restrictive leave policies;
2. family separation;
3. lack of command attention to personnel management and soldier welfare such as pay, housing, and promotions;
4. general dissatisfaction with military life;
5. tolerance of military and civil authorities toward desertion;
6. apparent public apathy toward the war;
7. increasingly heavy combat losses;
8. poor apprehension and punishment of offenders; and
9. misuse of certain types of units (especially Ranger and Popular Forces) by higher headquarters.

Desertions were especially prevalent in III Corps Tactical Zone because of the proximity of Saigon, where a deserter could readily lose himself. The nearby South Vietnam Army 5th Infantry Division alone lost 2,510 soldiers through desertion in the first quarter of 1966.

To attack the roots of the desertion problem, Military Assistance Command pressed many corrective programs and actions during the next several years. Among the more significant measures were the streamlining of administrative procedures, establishment of an Adjutant General's School, a liberal awards policy, improved leave policies, improved promotion system, battlefield promotions, direct appointments, and improvements in the standard of living for the South Vietnam Army to include pay increases and expansion of the commissary system, a self-help dependents housing program, and veterans rehabilitation programs. These activities had only mixed short-term success and by themselves represented only a part of the larger problem noted above.

Desertion rates tended to be confusing because the South Vietnam government classified as deserters those individuals with less than ninety days' service who were absent without leave (AWOL) more than six (later fifteen) days, and those who were absent more than fifteen days while en route to a new duty station. It was also suspected that desertion and recruiting statistics included some persons who had illegally transferred from one force to a more desirable one—for example, from the South Vietnam Army to the Popular Forces. Military Assistance Command had proposed substantial changes in this approach and recommended that a uniform period of thirty days unauthorized absence be the criterion; after that time the individual would be punished by the commander and a punishment book used to record the action. But Republic of Vietnam armed forces were unresponsive to these recommendations.

Orders published during 1965 removed all effective disciplinary restraint to desertion by allowing deserters to escape prosecution by signing a pledge not to desert again, after which, rather than being jailed, they were returned to duty. Before this step the armed forces code of military justice had provided strict penalties for desertion in wartime, ranging from six years imprisonment to death. The reduction in severity of punishment for desertion was partially explained by the overcrowded conditions of Vietnamese jails and Vietnamese unwillingness to levy harsh penalties for what was not considered a serious crime. But desertions from all components of the Vietnamese armed forces had risen from 73,000 in 1964 to 113,000 in 1965 and it seemed likely that this trend would continue in 1966.

To remedy this state of affairs, a series of decrees in April and

July established new penalties for deserters and their accomplices. First offenders would be punished by making them "battlefield laborers" for a minimum of five years; all pay, death, and disability benefits were forfeited. Battlefield laborers were to perform such duties as repairing roads and bridges, transporting ammunition, digging emplacements, burying the dead, setting up temporary camps, and in general performing hard labor details. Repeat offenders were to receive increased punishment; for a second offense, the penalty was five to twenty years hard labor; and if a deserter escaped while undergoing punishment, the punishment was doubled for the first offense and was death for the second. Civilians convicted of aiding and abetting deserters were to be sentenced to five years punishment at hard labor.

Emphasizing the gravity of the desertion problem and the importance he attached to the new laws, in July 1966 General Westmoreland sent a communiqué to all advisory personnel stating his conviction that "The present for operations strength of each unit must be raised. The minimum acceptable number to conduct a battalion operation is considered to be 450 men. The most important single improvement that can be made in the RVNAF to achieve this goal is a solution to the desertion problem; and to this end, advisory effort must be focused."

After a trip to the Van Kiep National Training Center in early July, the MACV J-1 reported that as a consequence of Vietnamese armed forces new AWOL and desertion measures, improvement was evident; no AWOL's or desertion occurred in the 2,000-man camp for the preceding seven days. Later, as the good results of the decrees became more apparent, the MACV commander congratulated the Chief, Joint General Staff, for the forceful and enthusiastic manner in which the desertion problem was being attacked. But privately, his optimism remained restrained.

Throughout the year the campaign continued to thrive. Posters highlighted the consequences of AWOL and desertion, and letters went to families of all deserters urging their return. On 8 August another desertion decree granted amnesty to individuals who had deserted from one force in order to join another and who were serving honorably in the force to which they had deserted.

In an effort to assist the South Vietnam Army reduce its desertion rate and improve its combat effectiveness, General Westmoreland directed that U.S. units adopt certain Vietnam Army units. Close association was planned between the U.S. 1st Infantry Division and the South Vietnam Army 5th Division and between the U.S. 25th Infantry Division and the South Vietnam Army 25th Division. The program was designed to provide U.S. help in establishing adequate exchange and commissary services, in erecting adequate dependent housing, and in combined tactical operations.

The USMACV also co-operated by preventing American civil and military agencies and contractors from hiring deserters. In October 1966, Military Assistance Command published a directive which required U.S. agencies to screen their employees for deserters and draft evaders, and which specified the documentation an individual had to present before he was hired. Since the directive did not apply to other Mission agencies, however, loopholes still existed. To plug these holes, the MACV commander asked the embassy to publish a similar directive which would apply to U.S. agencies not supervised by Military Assistance Command.

Throughout 1966 and 1967 progress was slow and painful. But through continued emphasis on the problem by advisers, together with the initiation of programs to attack the root causes of desertion (such programs, for example, as improving leadership, personnel, management, personnel services, and training) and stricter enforcement of desertion laws, a certain amount of headway was made. By the end of 1967 desertions had fallen by about 30 percent, and the desertion rate (per thousand) had dropped from the 16.2 of 1966 to 10.5. However, desertions continued to constitute one of the most critical problems facing the South Vietnam Army. Strong and continuous measures emphasizing the need for improvement of leadership, of the day-to-day living environment of the soldier and his dependents, and of the motivation and indoctrination of the citizen were mandatory if the rate was to be kept to an acceptable level.

Economic and Social Improvement

On 11 January 1967, the MACV commander met with his principal staff officers and component commanders to discuss means of improving South Vietnam armed forces effectiveness. The new role of the South Vietnam Army soldier in the pacification program emphasized the need to improve his lot in life. Obviously a program designed to improve the well-being of the people would not succeed if one of the main participants was worse off than those he was trying to help. At the time of the meeting, the four most important areas for consideration were field and garrison rations, food for South Vietnam Army dependents, cantonments, and dependent housing.

The South Vietnam armed forces pay system did not include a ration allowance; subsistence-in-kind or increased pay would have improved the system, but whatever measures were adopted had to be flexible enough to meet local conditions. U.S. help might be extended in several ways; one of the most practical was assistance-in-kind in the form of staples. The South Vietnam government would pay for the items, and the United States would use the money for expenses in South Vietnam. Captured rice was another source of rations. The MACV commander directed the commanding general of U.S. Army, Vietnam, to assume responsibility for improving field ration utilization, for garrison ration commodities, and for the distribution system. When the field ration was issued, 33 piasters (about 25 cents) was deducted from the soldier's pay; as this reduction lowered the food-buying power of the family man, he preferred not to receive the ration and sold it when it was issued to him. Thus the United States recommended that the ration be issued free of charge and in lieu of pay increases. The garrison ration consisted of certain basic foods distributed through South Vietnam armed forces quartermaster depots at fixed prices and locally procured perishables and was supported through payroll deductions. Only rice was occasionally short, and U.S. Army, Vietnam, requested that the South Vietnam government ensure that sufficient allocations of rice be made available to the Vietnamese armed forces. Also noteworthy was the establishment for the first time, on 21 February 1967, of unit messes in regular armed forces and Regional Forces company-size units.

U.S. Army, Vietnam, was also tasked with improving the armed forces commissary system with respect to the use of dependent food purchases and to consolidate the post exchange and commissary into one system. By early May negotiations for U.S. support of the Vietnamese armed forces commissary system had been concluded. The agreement stipulated that the United States would supply rice, sugar, canned condensed sweetened milk, canned meat or fish, cooking oil, and salt (or acceptable substitutes) for one year at a maximum cost to the United States of $42 million. The food items were to be imported into South Vietnam tax-free, for exclusive distribution through the armed forces commissary system. No food items were authorized for transfer to other South Vietnam government agencies, but would be sold only to armed forces personnel and their dependents at a cost which would be significantly less than on the open market, but still high enough to produce sufficient revenue to fund improvements to the system and to allow eventual U.S. withdrawal, and for its extension, if mutually agreeable. Piaster receipts from sales would remain the property of the commissary system and were not authorized for any other South Vietnam government agency; the government also agreed to provide the United States with a monthly financial statement. The agreement contained provisions for continuation of the system after U.S. withdrawal, if mutually agreeable. The formal accord was signed on 26 May by Commander, U.S. Military Assistance Command, Vietnam, and Chief, Joint General Staff, at Da Nang.

The Cantonment Program consisted of two parts; first, cantonments programed and funded in the government of Vietnam defense budget (50 percent government of Vietnam and 50 percent U.S. Joint Support Funds) and, second, the U.S.-sponsored cantonment construction plan which provided cantonments for the force structure increase units of fiscal years 1965, 1966, and 1967. The Vietnamese armed forces cantonment program was hampered somewhat by competition for limited matériel, labor, and transportation. The major difficulty was the lack of a master plan, compounded by possible changes in the location of South Vietnam armed forces units participating in pacification.

The Vietnamese armed forces Department of Housing Program had been initiated in April 1961 for soldiers below the grade of sergeant. In 1964 the program was expanded to include all ranks and a separate Regional Forces program was begun. No Popular Forces housing existed, since individuals normally resided in their own homes. The calendar year 1967 government of Vietnam defense budget contained 300 million piasters to complete previous building programs and to construct both officer and enlisted quarters; the houses to be erected with the 1967 funds were ten-family units, providing each family with a living area 3.5 meters by 10.5 meters. Spiraling costs were expected to limit new construction to no more than 3,000 units. On 11 January 1967 the MACV commander assigned the principal U.S. responsibility for the program to U.S. Army, Vietnam, while the MACV Directorate of Construction was responsible for co-ordinating policy and programs and for funding.

Force Structure Expansion

As mentioned briefly in Chapter II, Military Assistance Command had completed a study in the last half of 1964 addressing itself to the Vietnamese armed forces levels. The study had proposed two alternatives: alternative one provided for an increase of 30,339 men in the regular forces, 35,387 in the Regional Forces, and 10,815 men in the Popular Forces; and alternative two provided for an increase of 47,556 in the regular forces and identical increases in the Regional and Popular Forces. Alternative one was approved, with some modifications, on 23 January 1965, and force levels were fixed at 275,058 for regular forces, 137,187 for the

Regional Forces, and 185,000 for the Popular Forces. But by 13 April 1965, with no improvement in the military or political situation, alternative two increases were also approved and the regular force ceiling rose to 292,305. These increases were used to raise the number of South Vietnam Army infantry battalions from 119 (93 infantry, 20 Ranger, and 6 airborne) to 150. To avoid activating new headquarters units, one new infantry battalion was added to each Vietnam Army regiment (a later adjustment to 149 battalions was made when the activation of two additional airborne battalions took up the spaces of about three infantry battalions). Activation of these units began immediately, and by the end of the year twenty-four were either in the field or in training areas.

Planning and study of the force structure requirements was a continuous activity. By 5 November 1965, additional increases had been requested to provide for a regular force of 311,458 troops in fiscal year 1966 and 325,256 in fiscal year 1967. The fiscal year 1966 increases were primarily to flesh out the existing structure in the areas of command and control, psychological operations, and the replacement pipeline. Pipeline increases were needed to reduce the tendency to "fill" units with untrained personnel and allow the growing force structure a longer manpower lead time. As training became more complex, both longer lead times and greater pipeline increases would be necessary.

Increases for fiscal year 1967 included 3 infantry battalions (to replace those traded off for 2 airborne battalions in 1965), 1 infantry regiment, 1 artillery battery (105-mm.), 2 military police companies, 1 Marine battalion, 1 civil affairs company, 4 psychological warfare companies, 81 Regional Forces companies (to accommodate the expanding pacification program), and 15,000 spaces for the Regional Forces and other augmentations to increase the capability of existing Vietnamese armed forces units. Larger increases were needed, but the manpower situation would not make such increases possible. The U.S. Secretary of Defense gave his verbal approve for the new ceilings in Saigon on 28 November 1965.

The requested force increases represented the maximum strength that the manpower base could support. Accessions of 20,000 per month would be required to attain and sustain these levels; maintenance of these levels past 1969 would call for the recovery of significant manpower resources from Viet Cong controlled areas or the extension of military terms of service and recall of veterans. Manpower limitations were of course qualitative as well as quantitative. It was becoming increasingly difficult to obtain and train able leaders for the rapidly expanding forces.

The formation of new units continued throughout 1966. However, the general manpower shortage was making it difficult to sustain this high growth rate. A moratorium on the activation of new units was finally called, and the fiscal 1966 Vietnamese force structure was stabilized at a total strength of 633,645 consisting of 315,660 regulars (277,363 Army, 15,833 Navy, 7,172 Marine Corps, and 15,292 Air Force), 141,731 Regional Forces, and 176,254 Popular Forces.

Limits of Expansion

Discussions between Military Assistance Command and the Joint General Staff on the manpower situation during May and June 1966 explored the possibility of suspending unit activations called for in the fiscal year 1967 force structure. On 30 June General Westmoreland wrote the JGS chief that the objectives of the fiscal year 1967 force structure might not be attainable and should be re-examined to afford a more realistic alignment of forces as a means of increasing combat effectiveness. He cited desertions and unauthorized units as major causes for the unsatisfactory strength situation, and asserted that it was imperative for the activation of additional units to be suspended for the remainder of 1966. Units authorized for early activation to meet operational requirements were exempted from the suspension.

General Westmoreland's immediate concern was the declining present-for-combat strength of the Vietnamese Army infantry units. MACV studies showed that, as of 28 February 1966, South Vietnam Army divisions averaged 90 percent of authorized strength, and battalions averaged 85 percent. But only 62 percent of authorized strength was being mustered for combat operations in the field. There were two major reasons for this disparity. First, division and regimental commanders had organized a number of *ad hoc* units such as strike and reaction forces, reconnaissance and security units, and recruiting teams. Second, large numbers of deserters, long-term hospital patients, and soldiers killed in action continued to be carried on the rolls long after their names should have been deleted.

In reviewing the South Vietnam Army strength problem, planners particularly scrutinized unauthorized units. One type of unit found in almost all infantry regiments was the reconnaissance company. That a need existed for this kind of unit was indicated in a subsequent study. Approval was given to develop the organization for a regimental reconnaissance company which could be incorporated into the normal force structure.

In order to give his review efforts a broader base, Westmoreland tasked the U.S. Senior Advisors in each of the four corps tactical zones and other major armed forces components to initiate detailed support of the South Vietnamese organizations. Were they all being used according to their organizational mission, did they contribute effectively to the over-all mission, or could they be reduced in TOE strength, absorbed into other units, or deleted entirely? Replies from the field cited only a few examples of improper employment; in some instances such employment was caused by lack of proper equipment (for instance, armored cars in Regional Forces mechanized platoons), and in others it was due to local reasons (such as using reconnaissance companies as housekeeping units). In I Corps Tactical Zone the Senior Advisor felt that the Ranger battalions though not properly employed still were contributing to the war effort. In IV Corps Tactical Zone the only significant shortcoming noted was the continued use of provisional regimental reconnaissance companies. The survey located quite a few units which could be deleted entirely or which could be absorbed into other units. There were several inadequately trained scout companies which, if they failed to respond to organizational training, were recommended for deletion, conversion to Regional or Popular Forces, or absorption into other units. It was also recommended that armored units be absorbed into the regular infantry divisions. But in most cases the U.S. Senior Advisors felt that assigned Vietnamese Army units were necessary and contributed to the over-all mission.

In 1967, with the authorized force level still frozen at the fiscal year 1966–67 strength of 633,645, planning for fiscal year 1968 force levels began. On 26 April recommended fiscal year 1968 force levels were submitted and proved substantially higher than the present ceiling. The fiscal year 1968 program called for a total strength of 678,728 with the Vietnamese Army level at 288,908, Regional Forces at 186,868, and the Popular Forces at 163,088. Whether South Vietnam could support further increases was a question mark.

The development of fiscal year 1968 force structure was long and complex. Inflationary trends, South Vietnam government mobilization policies, the balance of forces, and especially the availability of manpower assets were considered. The new force level was based on an estimated population of 16,500,000; this number was considered sufficient to support the new levels through December 1968 but projections beyond that date were tenuous. A review conducted in late May tentatively identified additional spaces needed in the regular force, and the fiscal year 1968 force level was further increased to 685,739. The most important cause of these increases was the need for additional territorial (Regional and Popular Forces) units in areas recently brought under friendly control. Such expansion also increased the recruiting base, but the lag between the growth of the recruiting base and the growth of the Vietnamese Army was considerable. Thus the May review again addressed the question of whether these increases were attainable within the planned time frame, taking into account leadership potential, recruiting capability, equipment availability as well as available manpower and budgetary limitations. With certain augmentations, the training base and logistical support structure was considered adequate to support an increase in the force structure, but available leadership resources were likely to be severely strained. However, as before, to strain these resources appeared to be the more desirable alternative.

In July 1967 the Joint Chiefs of Staff asked that the revised fiscal year 1968 force level be reconciled with the earlier estimates. Military Assistance Command replied that the structure review had considered alternative force structures and various mixes of Regional and Popular Forces and regular forces. When examined within the context of projected U.S. troop deployments, anticipated enemy activities, and projected operational plans, the April estimate had proved too low. In addition, the fiscal year 1968 force levels were based on the assumption that the South Vietnam government would mobilize its manpower in January 1968 by lowering the draft age to nineteen, extending tours by one year, and recalling selected reservists. The U.S. Mission had long urged such measures and the JGS chief seemed to view the prospects favorably. While the Vietnamese armed forces manpower resources would support these levels, they were the maximum that could be sustained. The armed forces perennial leadership problem could be partially solved by retraining and calling up qualified and experienced combat leaders, phasing unit activations over a two-year period, and employing U.S. training teams with new Regional Forces companies. In the end, the revised fiscal year 1968 force level was confirmed and a force level of 685,739 (303,356 South Vietnam Army, 16,003 Navy, 7,321 Marine Corps, 16,448 Air Forces, 182,971 Regional Forces, and 159,640 Popular Forces) was authorized.

In October 1967 the Secretary of Defense approved the fiscal year 1968 force level of 685,739, contingent upon the implementation of the necessary manpower mobilization measures. But all activations were to be handled on a case-by-case basis until a joint MACV–JGS activation schedule could be developed and approved. The activation schedule would be dependent on manpower availability, recruiting experience, the continued development of leadership potential, the maintenance of adequate present-for-operations strength, the availability of equipment, and the capability of the support base. Again on 18 November the JGS chief was informed that many South Vietnam Army infantry units still had extremely low present-for duty or field strengths. But despite this situation, an activation scheduled for the new Army units was approved on 9 December 1967. At the end of 1967 actual South Vietnam armed forces strength was approximately 643,000. The new units to be activated between January and April 1968 made mandatory increased recruiting through new mobilization decrees.

In January 1967 General Westmoreland approved a step which he had vetoed only months before—withdrawal of MAP support from unproductive or ineffective Vietnamese army forces units. The MAP Directorate initiated a program aimed at identifying unproductive units, and in April it sent a letter to Chief, Joint General Staff informing him of the program and potential candidates to be deprived of support. The U.S. Navy planned to reduce its support of the South Vietnam Navy by $7,800 during fiscal year 1968 by discontinuing support for two ex-fishing boats because they were not slated to perform any mission assigned to the Vietnamese Navy. Other likely candidates from the Vietnamese Navy were underwater demolition teams not properly employed, and a light cargo ship which was used in a training role rather than in logistic support. The South Vietnam Army also had units nominated to have MAP support withdrawn. In II Corps Tactical Zone the 22d and 23d Ranger Battalions and in III Corps Tactical Zone the 5th Armored Cavalry Regiment had ineffective leadership and were assigned inappropriate missions. Restoration of support would be contingent upon institution of corrective action. Westmoreland wanted the program continued with a final evaluation of unproductive units every June and December; this action would give Vietnamese armed forces time to take remedial actions. Curtailing support to regimental headquarters companies could present serious problems, but a possible solution would be to inactivate the regiment and use its productive battalions elsewhere. Loss of a battalion was not desirable but, if necessary, a regiment could learn to operate with three battalions instead of the four that most had. General Westmoreland stated that Military Assistance Command was the administrator of U.S. funds and equipment and was responsible for ensuring productive utilization of U.S. resources.

The JGS chief wrote to the MACV commander on 3 May requesting that the Joint General Staff and the MACV staff work together to improve substandard units. The MACV commander concurred and directed the MACV staff to co-ordinate directly with the Joint General Staff in improving substandard Vietnamese armed forces units as they were identified. Since corrective measures had been initiated in the 22d and 23d Ranger Battalions and in the 5th Armored Cavalry Regiment, General Westmoreland decided to continue military assistance to them, but he proposed that the units be placed on probation until their effectiveness was conclusively established.

In early August the MAP Directorate identified additional Vietnamese armed forces units for possible withdrawal of MAP support. Eighteen Regional Forces companies, sixteen Popular Forces platoons, and fourteen Popular Forces squads constituted the majority of the unsatisfactory or marginal units. Besides these, two South Vietnam Army infantry battalions, an armored cavalry regiment, an engineer battalion, a reconnaissance troop, and an armored car platoon were identified as unsatisfactory. Deficient leadership, defective training, obsolete equipment, and meager personnel strength caused the low ratings. Deficient leadership was present in all but seven instances. One company commander was described as "seldom present" and "preoccupied with his own safety and comfort," while another was "absent for a two-month period due to self-inflicted leg wound." Obsolete equipment caused two poor ratings, and low personnel strength appeared in twenty-six others. Defective training programs accompanied deficient leadership in almost every instance. Further force increases were obviously contingent on whether Vietnamese armed forces leaders could bring their poorer units up to acceptable standards.

Territorial Forces

During this period both the missions and composition of the territorial forces became stabilized. The Regional Forces were voluntary units organized within a province for use within that province and consisted of rifle companies, river boat companies, and support units. The Popular Forces were voluntary locally recruited forces, organized into squads and platoons, used primarily as security forces in villages and hamlets. Regional Forces strength for fiscal years 1965 and 1966 had been set at 137,187 men organized into 759 companies; fiscal year 1967 force structure authorized 888 companies, an increase of 121 over fiscal year 1966, with a strength of 155,322 men. The emphasis on revolutionary development at the Honolulu conference meant that more Regional Forces companies would be needed to extend South Vietnam government influence into recently cleared areas or into national priority areas.

In order to gain lead time, 31 companies were scheduled for activation before 1 July, 21 were programed for national priority areas, and 10 for corps priority areas. The remaining fifty companies were scheduled for activation between July 1966 and June 1967.

General Westmoreland believed that the territorial forces were one of the keys to pacification, but felt they were not receiving enough attention from the South Vietnam government. U.S. financial support for continual larger force levels was not enough. The Regional and Popular Forces depended on volunteers to swell their ranks, and often such individuals joined only to escape the more burdensome service in the regular Army. As Vietnamese armed forces recruiting pressures grew more intense, however, competition for manpower increased and territorial strength declined in 1965 and 1966. High desertion rates of the territorial forces and recruiting restraints placed on them by the Joint General Staff in 1966 were the immediate causes. These restrictions prohibited the Popular Forces from recruiting men from twenty to twenty-five years of age; later in the year further bans prevented them from recruiting those in the seventeen to thirty bracket. To make matters worse, the restrictions were retroactive to 1 January 1966, making the status of some 17,000 recruits in the restricted age group illegal. Although these restrictions were later relaxed in September and the Popular Forces were authorized to retain the recruits in the retroactive category, the change came too late to compensate for the losses of the first nine months.

The Regional Forces and Popular Forces command and control structure presented another dilemma. Territorial forces constituted approximately 50 percent of the total South Vietnam armed forces structure, but, in view of their size, they enjoyed a much smaller proportion of support. They were far down in priority for training, equipment, and leadership, resulting in marginal or unsatisfactory ratings in almost every category of their activities. The root of the problem was the chain of command. The Regional and Popular Forces central headquarters, whose mission was to command and manage the Regional and Popular Forces units throughout the country, did not have operational control of the units (except for the seven Regional and Popular Forces national training centers); the actual control of the Regional and Popular Forces was exercised by corps and divisions through sector commands.

In September 1966 the government of Vietnam decided to integrate the separate Regional Forces and Popular Forces headquarters at the Joint General Staff, corps, division, sector, and subsector into the regular military commands at these echelons. Two advantages ensued from this arrangement: fewer people were required for staff duty, thus releasing personnel for duty in the field; also, the new arrangement would provide more efficient logistical support of Regional and Popular Forces units. The integration placed operations, administration, and support of the Regional and Popular Forces under the responsible tactical commanders throughout the armed forces and thus provided for a more unified effort throughout the chain of command. The organization also placed Regional and Popular Forces troops under the command of sector and subsector commanders; since these commanders were closely connected with pacification, it was thought likely that Regional and Popular Forces troops would be used in their proper role of pacification support. A new position, the Chief of Central Agency and concurrently Deputy Chief of Staff for Regional and Popular Forces at Joint General Staff of the South Vietnam armed forces, was formed and made responsible for recommending policy and guidelines for the Regional and Popular Forces. The reorganization was to take place in two stages and be completed by the end of the year. It was mid-1967, however, before the new command relationships had been sorted out and the more serious problems resolved.

Following the Manila conference, with its proposal to withdraw U.S. troops and Free World Military Assistance Forces from South Vietnam within six months, as the other side withdrew and stopped infiltrating, and as the level of violence subsided, Military Assistance Command noted that the conference communiqué did not provide for U.S. military advisory personnel to remain after a withdrawal. In these circumstances, besides strengthening the civilian components of the mission, it was considered prudent to consider immediate organization and training of a national constabulary under the guidance of Military Assistance Command. One suggestion was to draw upon Regional Forces and Popular Forces as a manpower source, while another was to designate the Regional Forces as a provincial police force and Popular Forces as a village police force. General Westmoreland agreed that early organization, with MACV assistance, of a constabulary was necessary to provide a force which would not be subject to negotiations. It appeared to Westmoreland, however, that direct military participation should be terminated as soon as possible. Several advantages were to be gained from building on the Regional and Popular Forces base, since those forces, besides constituting an organized force, already had an assigned mission which would not be changed substantially by conversion; other paramilitary forces could be readily integrated into the program as well.

To organize a constabulary required planning and study and

the development of a concept of organization and operation. To provide the planning and development, an interagency study group was formed. The group completed its work in December 1966 and recommended that a Rural Constabulary be formed, utilizing the Police Field Force as a base and opening up all manpower resources, including the armed forces, to recruitment. The study group also proposed using Popular Forces personnel as a recruiting base for pacification cadre. General Westmoreland, however, continued to support the concept of converting the Regional and Popular Forces into a territorial constabulary and pointed out the uselessness of pacification cadre without local security supplied by a strong popular force or its equivalent.

The Civilian Irregular Defense Group

At the beginning of 1966 only 28,430 CIDG personnel were enrolled in 200 companies, although a strength of 37,250 was authorized for both fiscal year 1966 and 1967, which would have allowed a total buildup of 249 companies.

In 1965 a U.S. study group formulated a detailed plan for converting the majority of CIDG companies to Regional Forces companies by the end of 1965 and the remainder by the end of 1966. On 15 September 1965, the Joint General Staff had agreed to the plan in principle, but recommended that the conversion be voluntary; the Joint General Staff recognized the desirability of incorporating all military and paramilitary organizations into the South Vietnam armed forces, but recognized that the unique role of Civilian Irregular Defense Group remained valid for the immediate future. In concept, as the areas in which CIDG units were operating became more suited for Regional Forces operations, the CIDG units would be converted to Regional Forces. U.S. and South Vietnamese Special Forces then would move to other locations and recruit and train other CIDG forces. General Westmoreland recommended slow and deliberate conversion, with the use of two or three camps as pilot models.

Initially, three camps were chosen for conversion: Plei Do Lim in Pleiku Province, Buon Ea Yang in Darlac Province, and An Phu in Chau Doc Province. Numerous delays ensued before the test was completed in August. Initial problems centered around the disadvantages of conversion to the participants: reduced resupply capability, since the U.S. Army Special Forces was no longer supplying the camp; a decrease in pay to some unmarried personnel when converted; and increased pressure on South Vietnam armed forces deserters who had joined the Civilian Irregular Defense

Group. When coupled with the traditional distrust of the Montagnards for the South Vietnam government, the unpopularity of conversion and its temporary suspension in 1966 was not surprising.

Training and Leadership

Paralleling the expansion of the South Vietnam armed forces massive efforts were made to improve the quality of the armed forces and training programs represented one of the most efficient ways to bring this about. While the old adage that units "learn to fight by fighting" is true, fighting alone was not enough. In Southeast Asia it was necessary to win and to keep winning a complex war where set-piece battles often gave only the illusion of victory. Thus, the advisory effort was devoted to creating not only an army that was tactically and technically proficient, but a professional one that could cope with the social, economic, and political turmoil in which it operated and from which it was derived.

The greatest obstacle in improving and training the armed forces was the lack of qualified leadership at all levels, both officer and noncommissioned officer. This deficiency had been a continuing source of concern and one which seriously affected all efforts to create an effective combat force. Battalion and company commanders were often inexperienced and lacked initiative; few operations were conducted in the absence of detailed orders. Senior commanders issued directives, but failed to supervise their execution, and results were usually negligible. U.S. advisers continually cited poor leadership as the foremost reason for unit ineffectiveness. But with the lack of replacements, unsatisfactory commanders were seldom relieved. This situation was an unfortunate by-product of the rapid expansion of the military without a strong base of experienced leaders; the shortage of able personnel to occupy civil administrative positions only made the military problem more severe.

Looking back on his career as Deputy Senior Advisor in II Corps Tactical Zone in 1966–67, Major General Richard M. Lee concluded that the basic problem

> was not a lack of knowledge or training facilities to do the job expertly, but a disinclination of many ARVN officers to take the time and effort to train their troops carefully and thoroughly. The Vietnamese had been intermittently at war since World War II with only an occasional respite; many ARVN officers looked at the war as a long pull rather than on a one-year basis, as we Americans tended to see our personal contributions. They tended to take the weekends off. They were not inclined to go in for the intensive training methods that the US forces were accustomed to at that time.

Lee went on to point out that many Vietnamese officers were not "training oriented" and also noted the class bias of the officer corps:

> It appeared to me that the ARVN officers as a group came from the middle and upper-educated classes of Vietnamese society, comprised primarily of a few of the old aristocracy, the officer group created by the French military during the Indo-China War, and the rising Commercial/business classes from the major cities, particularly Saigon. While there were many outstanding exceptions, surprisingly large numbers of this officer corps seemed to lack aggressiveness, leadership ability, and a full professional commitment to their profession. This had a pervasive, adverse impact on training. Considerable numbers of ARVN field officers seemed to prefer rear area assignment rather than combat command. Some sought political jobs (in provinces and districts), I reluctantly conclude, so that they could avoid the rigors, boredom, and dangers of training and combat, and a few (I suspect but cannot prove) [sought] to use their positions for personal or even financial advantage.

Lee ended this candid assessment by suggesting a democratization of the corps by "integrating and broadening the officer base, making it more egalitarian and opening a means of sought-after upward mobility."

Before July 1966, efforts to improve leadership were isolated and had met with little success. That month a Command Leadership Committee was formed consisting of the South Vietnam Joint General Staff chairman and five general officers. Under MACV guidance, the committee was charged with the formulation of comprehensive programs to improve leadership quality and personnel effectiveness throughout the Vietnamese armed forces. Several noteworthy actions resulted. A career management program for officers was implemented which provided for rotation of officers between command, staff, and school assignments, and the assignment of newly commissioned officers to combat units. The program was similar to the career management policies of the U.S. Army. In 1967 the Officer Annual Promotion Procedure incorporated efficiency reports into the selection process for the first time and opened the findings of the board to their military audience; the number of officers considered, the number selected, and the point average of each were all published. That same year, the Noncommissioned Officer Annual Promotion Procedure also made full disclosure to the field of the board's proceedings and considered noncommissioned officers strictly on their merits; unlike past practice, no consideration was given to unit noncommissioned officer strength, and imbalances were corrected through unit transfers after the promotion announcements had been made. A revised selection process for attendance at the Saigon Command and General Staff

THE BUILDUP YEARS, 1965-1967

TRAINING AT PHU CAT

College was instituted; student selections were made by the Joint General Staff rather than by allocating quotas to subordinate commands. The current position and promotion potential of candidates would weigh more significantly. A Vietnamese-authored *Small Unit Leaders Guide* was published containing sections on leadership, discipline, troop leading procedures, and company administration and was issued to all company commanders and platoon and squad

Range Practice With New M16 Rifle

leaders. A revitalization of the South Vietnam armed forces Inspector General system was also undertaken; reforms were patterned after the U.S. Inspector General system and incorporated personal complaint and redress procedures. Military Assistance Command provided sixteen Inspector General advisers to assist and monitor the effort. Finally a comprehensive Personnel Records Management Program was implemented in an effort to establish an accurate, responsive system for qualitative and quantitative identification of all personnel.

One of the unsatisfactory policies of Vietnamese armed forces was its commissioning system which heavily emphasized formal education, thereby eliminating the potential leadership ability in the enlisted ranks. Military Assistance Command strongly urged arrangements wherby qualified and deserving enlisted individuals might be commissioned from the ranks. The matter was extremely sensitive in a land where political and military power went hand in hand, but finally in 1966 three major steps were taken. First, a Special Officer Candidate Training Course was opened for enlisted men who had undergone two years of military service and had achieved the grade of corporal first class or higher. Six classes were held during the year and a total of 1,739 graduates were commissioned as aspirants. A second program resulted in the direct commissioning of 401 master sergeants first class in the regular force and 100 in the Regional Forces as aspirants. A third program awarded special battlefield commissions to 16 master sergeants first class in the regular forces and 4 in the Regional Forces. Thus by the end of the year these programs had awarded over 2,000 commissions to servicemen from the ranks and set valuable precedents for succeeding years.

The schools and training centers also felt the new demand for leadership. Service school curriculums were revised to provide more intense leadership training, especially the Vietnamese Military Academy which remained the primary source for regular officers and which had now been permanently expanded from a two-year course to a four-year degree-granting institution. Officer candidate courses as well as courses at branch schools were similarly broadened to meet the increased requirements for trained leaders, technicians, and specialists.

With U.S. assistance, improvements made in the Command and General Staff College consisted of program of instruction revisions, a guest lecture program, student lecture and research requirements, methods of instruction course for instructors, and a modern library index system. For leaders at the Saigon level, a National Defense College was established in August 1968 and devoted itself to educating higher ranking military officers and career government civilians.

In the National Training Center, a leadership development program was integrated into the normal South Vietnam Army recruit training. The top 10 percent of each South Vietnam Army basic/advanced individual training company was retained at the training center and given an additional three weeks training in leadership and small unit tactics. Upon completion, these students were assigned positions as squad and platoon leaders for the next two training cycles. Trainees who continued to excel were then selected for either the Noncommissioned Officer Academy or the Officer Candidate School.

Offshore Training

In 1965 and 1966 the offshore schooling program began to encounter a great deal of personnel trouble. The immediate cause was the high number of offshore schooling cancellations during the first three months of 1966; of a total of 366 servicemen scheduled for offshore schooling, 90 had had their spaces canceled. The main reason for the cancellations was the language qualification. These cancellations in turn interrupted the orderly progress of the program and created delays that could not be solved by mere rescheduling. Also, when the matter was reviewed in 1966, Military Assistance Command found that little had been done to study the long-term use made of these trainees after they returned to South Vietnam.

To remedy these ills, the MACV Training Directorate developed a system encompassing both U.S. and advisory chains of command. Of primary importance was the identification of candidates. Advisers and Vietnamese armed forces commanders were required to submit justification for schooling requests and the job assignments following its completion. Specific responsibilities for both the Vietnamese and the Americans were defined in a joint MACV-JGS directive. Increased efforts were also made to improve English language instruction and testing, and a new English language screening test was developed to supplement the English language comprehensive level test. The supplementary test was to be given six months before attendance at the course. These measures proved successful and by the end of the year well over 90 percent of the programed spaces were being utilized, but continued vigilance was necessary to ensure that the trained personnel were used in a proper manner.

South Vietnam Schools

On 13 December 1966, Premier Nguyen Cao Ky signed a decree permanently converting the Vietnamese Military Academy from a two-year to a four-year institution. (*Map 1*) Classroom instruction and curriculums were to be patterned after West Point. The Chief, Joint General Staff, initially opposed the curriculum which featured electrical and mechanical engineering and the social sciences and recommended one which emphasized electrical engineering with a lower priority given to mechanical and civil engineering. The superintendent, the academic dean, and the U.S. advisers at the Vietnamese Military Academy opposed this view and the school adopted a compromise curriculum.

On 13 February at the start of the academic year, the senior class of the Military Academy voluntarily split two classes: one moved into the four-year curriculum, the other remaining with the two-year program. Before 1967, cadets had been graded only semiannually in academic studies, and classes were based largely on lectures, with a minimum of outside study required. Beginning in

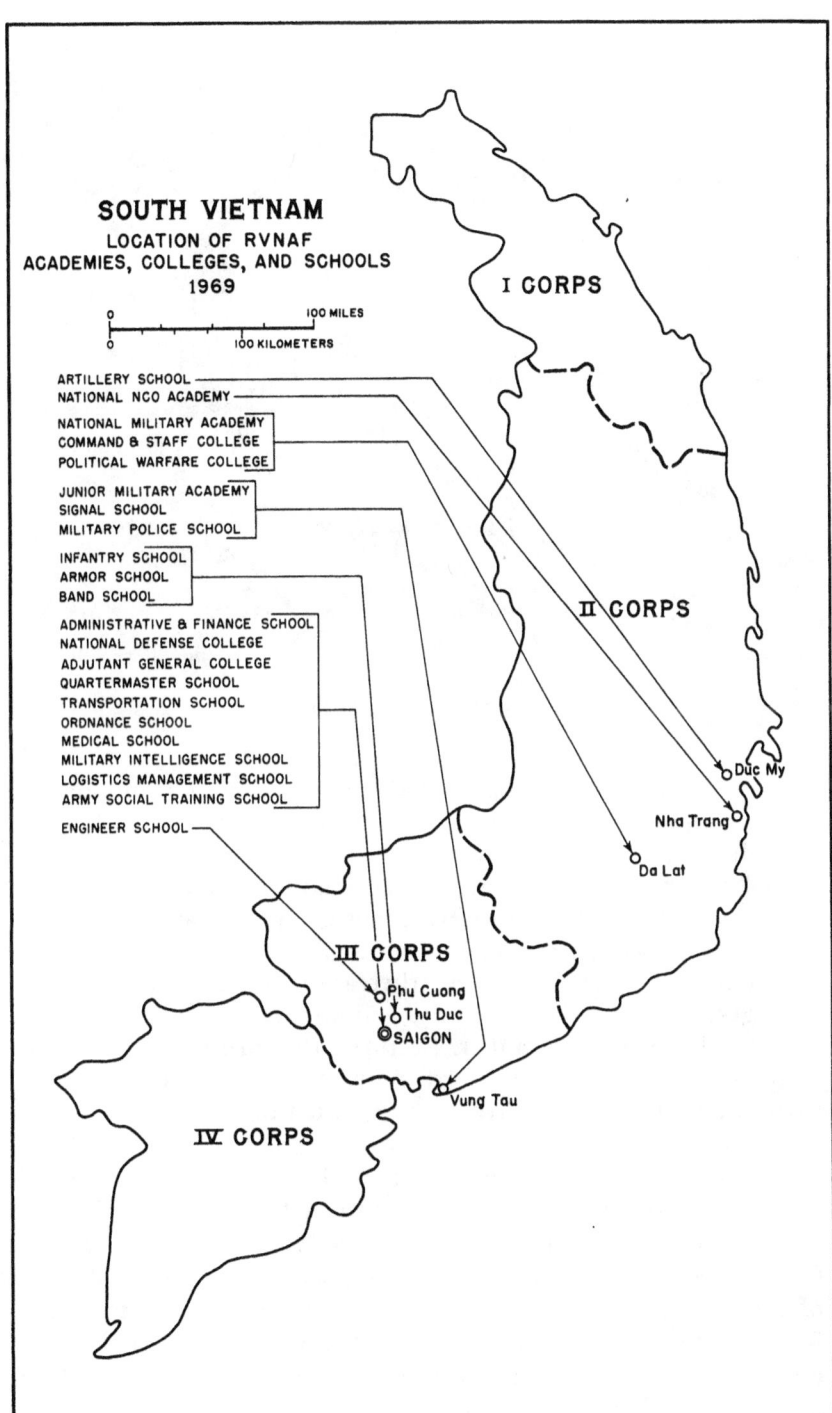

MAP 1

CADETS AT DALAT

February, cadets were graded daily in mathematics and physical sciences and graded weekly in the social sciences. The academic dean held a master's degree from the U.S. Naval Postgraduate School and believed strongly in the study and teaching methods used at West Point. Grades were posted weekly and the first resectioning, based on academic standing, occurred on 1 April and was continued every six weeks thereafter. Written partial exams were given biweekly or monthly, and written general exams were given in June and November. Lectures, the former mainstay, were frowned upon, and cadets were required to study three hours a night after an average of five hours' instruction daily.

U.S. officer adviser strength was increased from six to thirteen to furnish a well-qualified advisor to each of the eight academic departments. General Westmoreland strongly supported the Vietnamese Military Academy, noting in a letter to the Chief, Joint General Staff, that "continued development of the VNMA is one of the most important programs currently in progress to provide for the future of the Republic of Vietnam. I feel that it should be given high priority and continued command interest and emphasis."

The expansion of the Military Academy into a four-year degree-granting institution continued throughout the remainder of calendar year 1967. Funds were made available for the modification of the academic building and the purchase of furniture. More than 570 slide rules were provided from U.S. sources, the sum of $52,000 was approved to assist in funding the translation and printing of textbooks, and two English language laboratories were made available through the Military Assistance Program. Plans for the construction of faculty quarters were also approved. The academic college advanced in the area of cadet extra instruction, valid semester examinations, department programs of instruction and standing operation procedures, and textbook selections. The new construction program continued to receive emphasis and work progressed on the difficult task of defining the design criteria for the massive laboratory building. The calendar year 1967 recruiting program for prospective cadets received special emphasis, including radio and television appeals. This program resulted in a 49 percent increase in applicants over 1966 (416 for 280 spaces).

In January General Westmoreland approved a study of the Command and General Staff College which discussed its chief drawbacks: a poor reputation, poorly qualified students, a faculty with marginal qualifications, and a lack of training funds. The Chief, Joint General Staff, did not accept completely the findings of the study and directed the Central Training Agency (CTA) to make a separate survey. The CTA study was completed in February and, although it differed from the MACV study on several major points, Westmoreland agreed to its findings and put its recommendations into effect in March. Selection of students was centralized at the Central Training Agency rather than delegated to corps, and only qualified officers with career potential were selected. Furthermore the training agency began assigning recent Vietnamese graduates of the U.S. Army Command and General Staff College as instructors and increasing the length of the courses taught. The college continued to improve its program and produced top Vietnamese graduates throughout 1967. Other college support improvements consisted of a college five-year plan, a college standing operation procedure, detailed budget studies for calendar years 1968 and 1969, and renovation of storage and supply facilities. Hours of instruction that were not pertinent to the situation in South Vietnam were reduced and the courses streamlined.

Considerable headway was made in establishing a National Defense College. A qualified Senior Advisor and two assistants were assigned to work with the JGS Central Training Agency as well as with a USAID-provided civilian educator in developing plans for the school. A committee of U.S. officers was appointed to work with the Joint General Staff to expedite the establishment of the school, and Westmoreland was optimistic about meeting a February 1968 opening date. Finding qualified persons was difficult, but Premier Ky signed the decree establishing the National Defense College on 23 August 1967 and made funds available for rehabilitation of the site chosen. The faculty then consisted of two Vietnamese officers, and initially only two courses were planned: a National Defense Course and a Senior Officers Seminar. The former lasted ten months, with the student body consisting of twenty senior military officers (lieutenant colonel, colonel, and brigadier general) and key government civilians. The Senior Officers Seminar met each Saturday and was attended by general officers and very senior civilians. The advisory detachment consisted of four officers, one noncommissioned officer, two enlisted men, and two local nationals. MAP support funds were approved by the Commander in Chief, Pacific, for procurement of equipment.

Despite all the effort devoted to building, supporting, and improving the training of the Vietnamese armed forces, the result was still a major question mark at the end of 1967. Certainly improvements had been made. A tenth infantry division had been activated and many combat support and combat service support units formed; training at national and corps training centers and the military schools had continued with comparatively few interruptions. But desertion rates were still too high, refresher training practically nonexistent, equipment too old, and statistical measurements of combat effectiveness untrustworthy. Only future performance in the field would serve as an adequate gauge of U.S. efforts since 1965 and by the end of 1967 that test was only months away.

CHAPTER IV

Vietnamization, 1968–1972

Background

South Vietnam was the test case for implementing the Nixon doctrine and a new U.S. planning approach to Asia. Vietnamization was both a goal and the program through which that goal would be achieved at the earliest practical time. The constituent elements of Vietnamization—improvement and modernization of the South Vietnam armed forces, pacification, and combat operations—were inseparably interwoven, and the United States made every effort to maintain and strengthen their natural interdependence. Within the context of the situation in South Vietnam, Vietnamization referred only to that portion of the war effort engaged in by the United States and did not refer to the total war effort which the government of Vietnam had carried as a large and heavy burden for so many years.

The 1968 *Tet* offensive aimed at inflicting a decisive defeat on allied military forces and at sparking popular uprisings against the South Vietnam government throughout the country. In a radical departure from his former strategy, the enemy brought his forces out of their cross-border sanctuaries, went to unprecedented lengths to assemble supplies and weapons, and infiltrated his local forces into the major cities and towns, while holding his main forces in reserve to exploit the anticipated uprisings. But the local Viet Cong units were expended in vain and the regulars fared no better. Only in Hue did the enemy succeed in holding out for more than a few days; in most areas, his guerrilla units and clandestine governments came out into the open only to be quickly destroyed. South Vietnamese units, including the territorial forces, stood firm and worked side by side with U.S. units to throw the enemy out of his objective areas. Far from weakening the government of Vietnam, the *Tet* attacks gave it a new unity and sense of purpose. It had suffered the enemy's worst attacks and survived.

Mobilization

The *Tet* offensive galvanized the Vietnamese mobilization effort. Having weathered the storm, government officials emerged with increased confidence and prestige, as well as with an increased sense of responsibility. American troop strength was now reaching its highest peak, and both Saigon and Washington began to feel public pressure for U.S. troop withdrawals. It was *Tet* that ushered in the era of Vietnamization. Immediately after the offensive, reservists with less than five years of active service were made subject to recall, and by 1 April 1968 nineteen-year olds were being drafted and by 1 May eighteen-year olds. Stronger enforcement efforts than ever were exerted as units sought to fill their depleted ranks. Finally, on 19 June, the South Vietnamese government announced a general mobilization and the interim period of mobilization by decree came to an end. Henceforth, personnel in the military service would serve an indefinite period as long as a state of war existed. All males between the ages of sixteen and fifty would be mobilized; those between eighteen and thirty-eight would serve in the armed forces (including the Regional and Popular Forces), and other age groups would serve in the new People's Self-Defense Force, a part-time, local militia. The government now had the confidence and the stability both to enact and enforce these strong measures.

The general mobilization succeeded in producing large numbers of recruits for the armed forces. During 1968, 80,443 men were conscripted into the armed forces and, under pressure of the draft, many others volunteered for units and stations of their own choosing. An accelerated pacification campaign in the closing months of the year brought 76.3 percent of the population within government security by the end of the year (with 11.4 percent contested and 12.3 percent still under Viet Cong control), a proportion never before equaled. This increase in turn further enlarged the government's recruiting base and made the continuing expansion of the armed forces possible.

Force Structure

Force structure planning continued, and in March 1968 Military Assistance Command, Vietnam, submitted new strength proposals for Washington approval. The proposals recommended a supported force level for the Vietnamese armed forces from the fiscal year 1968 approved level of 685,739 to a new level of 779,154 (including 341,869 Army, 211,932 Regional Forces, and 179,015 Popular Forces) in fiscal year 1969 and 801,215 (355,135 Army, 218,687 Regional Forces, and 179,015 Popular Forces) for fiscal year 1970. These increases provided for 1 regimental headquarters, 2 battalion headquarters, 4 infantry battalions, 15 artillery bat-

Rangers Defend Saigon, *TET* 1968

talions (105-mm.), 2 armored cavalry squadrons, increases in Regional and Popular Forces strength, additional logistical units, increases in pipeline authorizations, and increases in the South Vietnam Navy, Marine Corps, and Air Force. The proposed levels would further round out and balance the force structure and make significant progress toward developing a self-sustaining force capable of expanding or contracting its main effort to conform to shifts in the course of the war. Planning for these levels was done within the constraints of manpower availability, leadership potential, and inflationary pressures. As before, the major limiting factor was manpower availability.

In April 1968 the agreement between the governments of the United States and North Vietnam to begin peace talks brought a new sense of urgency to the development of the South Vietnam armed forces. Since its inception, the armed forces had been developed predominantly as a ground combat force. The United States had provided the major part of the air and naval effort, as well as essential general logistical support. But the prospect of an immediate negotiated withdrawal of U.S. and North Vietnamese forces required a radical departure from this role.

On 16 April the Deputy Secretary of Defense ordered a plan developed for gradually shifting the burden of the war to the South Vietnam forces and to support, as quickly as possible and to the maximum extent feasible, the efforts of the government of

Vietnam to enlarge, improve, and modernize the armed forces. In an almost simultaneous action, the Joint Chiefs of Staff asked for approval of an immediate force level increase to 801,215 men (regular and Regional and Popular Forces). On 28 May the new ceiling was approved, but funds were withheld pending a thorough examination of South Vietnam armed forces needs.

In late May the Vietnamization plan requested in April was also submitted. Essentially it proposed the dissolution of one Vietnamese Army infantry division to support necessary increases in naval, air, and logistical support units. But the following month the Defense Department approved only the equipment modernization and force structure increases in ground combat units and helicopter squadrons contained in the fiscal year 1968 portion of the plan. The Defense Secretary directed that a further review of the fiscal year 1969–70 portions be completed in order to prepare two contingencies or "phases." Phase I would be based on American participation in the war continuing at the current level; Phase II would provide for the development of a self-sufficient South Vietnam armed forces capable of coping with the internal insurgency that would remain after a joint U.S.–North Vietnamese withdrawal. No consideration was to be given now to the threat of the renewal of external aggression.

On 27 August Military Assistance Command, Vietnam, completed its Phase I Improvement and Modernization Program. Essentially, it provided for an armed force of 801,215, as requested by the JCS, and closely resembled the initial plan submitted in May. The Phase I Improvement and Modernization Program was based on two assumptions—first, barring a negotiated settlement, that the enemy threat would continue at the current level for an indefinite period, and, second, assuming continued U.S. participation at currently approved levels, that the South Vietnam armed forces did not need to be "balanced" since their lack of adequate air, naval, and logistical capability could be offset by U.S. support. The expansion of the armed forces naval and air elements would thus be restricted, and the Army logistical elements would receive only the minimum number of spaces required for effective support of combat units. Most increases would thus be devoted to ground combat forces and would ease problems stemming from artillery and armor deficiencies, unfilled division structures, inadequate direct support capability, and the lack of helicopter lift. The Phase I plan was quickly approved on 23 October 1968.

By September 1968, armed forces strength stood at 811,509, some 10,000 over the authorized force level, and the momentum of the general mobilization would soon carry this figure to over

850,000. Military Assistance Command consequently recommended that additional units be activated. An increase in the supported force ceiling would maximize the benefits of the mobilization, deny manpower to Viet Cong recruiters, and permit initiation of long lead-time training required to expedite the ultimate transition from a Phase I to a Phase II force structure. Military Assistance Command thus proposed that 48,785 more spaces be allocated and apportioned between the Regional Forces (39,000) and the pipeline (9,785). On 5 November Washington approved this request, and the new force levels for a Modified Phase I Improvement and Modernization plan rose to 850,000.

On 8 October Military Assistance Command submitted its plan for the balanced Phase II Improvement and Modernization force structure. The Phase II plan called for a force of 855,594 with substantial increases included for the Vietnamese Navy and Air Force. While this plan was being reviewed, on 9 November, the MACV commander requested authority to go beyond Phase I and move rapidly toward the Phase II posture. He considered that the Phase I plan was no longer in line with the situation in Vietnam and the political considerations associated with the negotiations being conducted in Paris. At the time, the U.S. government had suspended the air offensive against North Vietnam and, with a presidential election being held, there were increased expectations for progress at the peace talks. What was needed was the authority to proceed with the necessary programing, budgeting, and other actions required to provide manpower and equipment for the Phase II structure. The new commander of the U.S. Military Assistance Command in Vietnam, General Creighton W. Abrams, therefore recommended immediate approval of an Accelerated Phase II Improvement and Modernization plan and an immediate increase in force levels to 877,895 in order to make possible increased training or pipeline strength, with no immediate decrease in the scheduled expansion of the ground combat forces. The combat units could be phased down later once the emergency had run its course. The Joint Chiefs of Staff concurred and, except for the section on naval structure, the Deputy Defense Secretary approved the Phase II plan on 18 December, raising supported force levels to a new high of 866,434 and requesting Accelerated Phase II activation schedules as well as plans for withdrawal of U.S. units no longer needed after equipment turnover to South Vietnamese units. Approval of a modified naval structure on 12 February 1969 resulted in a total force of 875,790.

At the Midway conference in June 1969, the South Vietnam government requested support for further force increases and equipment modernization. At the time, major U.S. redeployments were being announced, enemy activity was low, and both pacification and mobilization efforts were going well. The proposals were partially supported by Military Assistance Command and the Joint Chiefs of Staff, and on 12 August the Secretary of Defense approved the "Midway package" which raised the total force level for fiscal year 1970 to 953,673. As before, the largest increases went to the territorial forces, which could be trained quickly and which were needed to provide security for recently pacified areas. On 6 January 1970, the Secretary of Defense approved the accelerated activation of Regional Forces and Popular Forces units in fiscal year 1970, increasing the Vietnamese armed forces level to 986,360.

During these developments, a more thorough study was undertaken to determine the final form of the armed forces once U.S. troops had withdrawn. Termed Phase III or the Consolidation Phase of the Republic of Vietnam Armed Forces Improvement and Modernization Program, its main objective was to identify and plan for long-range needs up to fiscal year 1973. In general, these needs reflected qualitative rather than quantitative improvement in the armed forces, and under the Phase III plan the total force structure would rise only moderately from the 986,560 Midway package for fiscal year 1970 to 1,100,000 by the end of fiscal year 1973. Most of the later force increases provided for more combat support and combat service support units as well as for territorial forces. On 5 June 1970 the Secretary of Defense approved the general outline of the Phase III plan, and thereafter specific items of the plan were approved in fiscal year increments, underwent continual review, and were altered as new needs were identified and older ones disappeared.

By 1972 most of the Phase III plan was completed, and both U.S. and Vietnamese armed forces efforts were concentrated on improving existing units and making comparatively minor adjustments within the over-all force structure. The only major force reorganization occurred in 1971 when an eleventh infantry division was formed in I Corps Tactical Zone. The constituent units, taken from two other divisions and local territorial forces, had little opportunity to co-operate before the North Vietnam Army offensive in the spring of 1972, and this lack may in part explain the poor performance of these units.

At the beginning of 1972 South Vietnamese combat strength was formidable: about 120 infantry battalions in 11 divisions supported by 58 artillery battalions, 19 battalion-size armored units, and many engineer and signal formations. On the front line were thirty-seven Ranger border defense battalions (mostly former CIDG units) and in reserve, twenty-one Ranger battalions and both the airborne and the Marine divisions. This powerful force of almost 429,000 men (South Vietnam Army and Marine Corps) was supported by a Navy of 43,000 men operating 1,680 craft and an Air Force of 51,000 men flying well over 1,000 aircraft, including about 500 helicopters.

The territorial force became stabilized at about 300,000 Regional Forces and 250,000 Popular Forces men, marshaled into about 1,679 Regional Forces companies and 8,356 Popular Forces platoons. The Regional Forces group and later Regional Forces battalion headquarters and administrative and direct support logistic companies were created to assist sector and subsector headquarters in managing these growing forces; however, the trend toward incorporating them into larger units—brigades and divisions—was generally resisted successfully.

Concurrent with the post-1968 expansion of the Vietnamese armed forces were significant increases in the paramilitary forces. Pacification personnel (RD, ST, and VIS cadres and armed propaganda teams) peaked in 1971, provincial reconnaissance units remained stable, and both the U.S.-employed Kit Carson Scouts and Civilian Irregular Defense Group were slowly phased out. The latter were eventually either disbanded or converted into border Regional Forces and Ranger units and incorporated into the regular Army. The greatest expansion in supported levels occurred in the National Police forces which rose from 16,900 in 1962 to 116,000 and in the local militia which rose from 1 million in 1969 to more than 4 million by 1970. It should be noted that the militia forces were at best part-time personnel, and their organization, the People's Self-Defense Force, represented an attempt to involve all levels of the population in the war effort, whatever their military value.

Desertions

In 1967 the South Vietnam armed forces desertion rate had been reduced to 10.5 per thousand, but efforts to lower this figure still further were unsuccessful. Traditionally, desertions had always increased just before the *Tet* holidays and 1968 was no exception. As before, the Joint General Staff asked all commanders to co-operate in minimizing this practice and tasked the Central Political Warfare Agency with publicizing news reports on trials of deserters by radio, television, newspapers, and magazines. Other measures were to make examples of typical offenders, to impose severe sentences, and to hold mobile court sessions. In addition, the agency prepared special radio broadcasting and TV programs for servicemen on New Year's Day. Annual leaves were to be granted on New Year's Day only to outstanding individuals who had a number of children, and units were still enjoined to remain within the established 5 percent leave system.

These measures notwithstanding, a considerable number of soldiers were absent from their units at the start of the enemy's *Tet* offensive and, in the heavy fighting that followed, absenteeism rapidly increased. The monthly desertion rates continued to rise to 16.5 per thousand in July (13,056 deserters), the highest count of any month since mid-1966, and reached an all-time high of 17.2 per thousand in October. Then, as the fighting subsided at the end of 1968 and in 1969, the desertion rate fell and again became stable at about 12 per thousand. Of course, all these rates were normally doubled and tripled in the individual tactical infantry units where most of the burdens of war were felt.

This time the South Vietnam government acted quickly to keep the rate at acceptable levels. On 27 September the Joint General Staff dispatched a directive establishing "quotas" or acceptable maximum rates of desertion for all commands. The directive stated that failure to meet these standards would result in the punishment or relief of commanders. Other measures followed. In October the Joint General Staff directed an increase in the award of the Gallantry Cross, primarily for lower ranks in combat units to include the Regional and Popular Forces, raised the number of personnel authorized to be on leave from 5 to 10 percent, and granted a graduation leave of ten days to those completing basic training (over and above the fifteen days of leave authorized annually). In addition, all sectors (provinces), special sectors, and special zones were told to organize guidance sections to aid personnel on leave and to include transient billets, messing, and transportation arrangements.

The South Vietnam armed forces also participated in the implemention of the National Police Records System. This system provides for the establishment of a central fingerprint file with a related system for furnishing information on all "wanted" personnel. The target date for completion of the fingerprinting of all the men in the South Vietnam armed forces was 31 January 1969. This program assisted in the identification and apprehension of deserters, especially those who deserted to enlist in other units.

Despite these new measures, the problem of desertion in the Vietnamese armed forces, and particularly within the Army and Marine Corps, was a matter of continuing command concern to

Military Assistance Command and the Joint General Staff. South Vietnam armed forces gross desertions for 1968 totaled 139,670 and were still the largest single cause of manpower loss. As a result of JGS antidesertion program in 1969, some progress was made and the number of deserters dipped to 123,311. In 1970 gross desertions were 150,469; however, 23,716 returned for a net loss of 126,753. This pattern, with no apparent trend, continued in 1971.

Pay and Allowances

The low base pay and allowances set for the men in the armed forces had a direct influence on desertions and morale. The base pay for single individuals was well below the average standard of living pay scale in Vietnam, and in August 1971 single members were accounting for 65 percent of the total desertions in combat units. The South Vietnam government had taken token action early in the year to provide incentive pay for combat personnel. On 9 February the South Vietnam Prime Minister prescribed a temporary special allowance of 100 piasters (37¢) per day military personnel and for the Ministry of Defense civilians who were participating in operations and support missions outside South Vietnam. On 8 March the government increased the cost of living allowance for regular forces and Regional Forces by 100 piasters per month for each service member, his legal wife, and each of his supported children. The base pay for members of the Popular Forces was increased by 100 piasters per month, and the cost of living allowance for his legal wife and each of his supported children was increased by a similar amount.

Recognizing that a substantial pay increase was needed for the armed forces and government employees, Military Assistance Command, Vietnam, in co-ordination with the U.S. Embassy and U.S. Agency for International Development, conducted a study of the armed forces pay scales during August 1971. Addressing the grave problem of procurement and retention within the combat infantry battalions, Military Assistance Command recommended across-the-board percentage increases (28 percent) in base pay, incentive pay for the South Vietnam Army combat units (4,500 piasters) and Regional Forces mobile battalions (2,000 piasters), and an increase in death gratuity payments. General Abrams submitted the pay proposal to the Minister of National Defense in September 1971, and the following November the government increased the cost of living allowance for all service members and civil servants by

1,200 piasters ($2.80) per man per month and authorized incentive pay as proposed by Military Assistance Command.

Subsequently the Chief, Joint General Staff, sought the MACV commander's assistance in seeking to obtain 4,500 piasters ($11.00) incentive pay for other "crack troops" who were excluded from the framework of the new pay measure. In response, General Abrams counseled that "in determining the best application of the military pay raise, primary consideration was given those units [combat infantry battalions] experiencing grave procurement and retention problems" and "any deviation to the current list [of authorized units] would be in contradiction of the stated purpose of the allowance and invite requests for exceptions from other services and arms." However, on 15 December the South Vietnam government's Ministerial Decree 1215 extended the incentive pay, without the MACV commander's sanction, to reconnaissance companies, shock companies, and scout companies subordinate to the 81st Ranger Group (Airborne) and to certain personnel assigned to the technical directorates.

Veteran Affairs

In the past, poor treatment of veterans had only exacerbated the problem of desertion. Traditionally, the Vietnamese armed forces carried physically impaired servicemen on the active rolls because of inadequate facilities for their physical and vocational rehabilitation; this practice caused a drawdown on unit present-for-operations strength. The Cat Lai Project, established May 1967, under the joint sponsorship of the Ministry of Defense and the Ministry of Veteran Affairs, conducted vocational school training for physically impaired personnel before discharge from the service, thus preparing them more adequately for civilian life. The goal was to train annually some 1,200 soldiers who, upon successful completion of their course, would be eligible for gainful employment. In July 1967 the school officially opened with 138 students enrolled in eight courses (tailoring, supply, mechanics, carpentry, plumbing, masonry, typing, and electronics), and in December it graduated ninety-five of the original students. Placement of these graduates by the Veterans Affairs Placement Office at first proved unsatisfactory; through the efforts of Education Consultants, Ltd., however, many of the students were later placed in civilian jobs.

In a letter to the Ministry of Defense on 4 January 1968, General Westmoreland reaffirmed his interest in the placement of physically impaired South Vietnam armed forces soldiers upon discharge from the service. A viable veterans program was an essential element of an effective armed force. On 16 January 1968, at a conference held to discuss the revitalization of the South Vietnam government Veterans Program, Westmoreland announced that Military Assistance Command would assume responsibility for advising and assisting the Ministry of Veteran Affairs in its Veterans Program and outlined four areas of concentration: hospitalization, classification, training, and job placement. He assigned the mission of implementing MACV's advisory effort to MACV J–1; this staff agency, in turn, formed a separate division whose mission was to advise the Ministry of Veteran Affairs in carrying out the objectives outlined by Westmoreland. In July this division was replaced by the Mobilization and War Veterans Advisory Branch in the Advisory Division of Military Assistance Command.

At first the advisory effort centered around the identification of resources, the determination of requirements, and the unification of all agencies affiliated with armed forces veterans affairs. Plans and material for the conduct of the command survey of physically impaired soldiers were prepared and made available to the Ministry of Defense and the Ministry of Veteran Affairs. Finally, a combined committee comprised of representatives from the Ministry of Defense, Ministry of Veteran Affairs, and Military Assistance Command was organized to formulate plans and administer the over-all program for armed forces physically impaired soldiers. In the area of hospitalization, aid was expected in getting additional hospital beds. Tied closely with hospitalization was a re-emphasis on the methods and execution of medical classification to ensure precise and prompt categorizing of the individual. When vocational training was prescribed, the accurate and rapid filing of occupational questionnaires and the issuance of a security clearance were imperative. In the case of individuals who desired civil employment, assurance of an early release became essential. Military authorities felt that by joining the Ministry of Defense, Ministry of Veteran Affairs, and Military Assistance Command, cooperation in these areas, policies beneficial to the individual, the armed forces, and the nation would be assured.

The development of private businesses was discussed with members of the Industrial Developments Branch of the U.S. Agency for International Development who were especially knowledgeable in this area. It was their opinion that industrial development planning should remain within the sphere of the Ministry of Economy, since its mission was to explore ventures of this nature. The MACV commander agreed with this position.

One important step forward was a South Vietnam government

Instruction at Da Nang Vocational School

reorganization which resulted in the merger of the Ministry of Defense and the Ministry of Veteran Affairs. The Ministry of Veteran Affairs lost its ministerial status and became an integral part of the Ministry of Defense which was redesignated Ministry of Defense and War Veterans. No changes in the administration and operation of the defunct ministry were anticipated.

In the area of job placement, the establishment of working relationships and close liaison between the job placement section, Ministry of Defense and War Veterans, and U.S.-Vietnamese civilian and governmental enterprises opened the way for the employment of physically impaired soldiers and veterans. During the second quarter of 1968, approximately 1,100 job referrals and placements were made. In an effort to create additional employment, the Ministry of Defense and War Veterans studied the feasibility of establishing factories to produce operational rations, ammunition, and items of organizational equipment. Additionally, the Ministry of Defense and War Veterans, working in conjunction with the Ministry of Economy, planned to utilize approximately 1,000 disabled veterans as security guards to relieve the Regional and Popular Forces guarding industrial complexes. These disabled soldiers would ultimately be discharged from the service and hired immediately by the industries concerned.

Leadership

The problems of leadership, promotions, and grade were interrelated and deserve special attention. In general, the actual grade structure of Vietnamese armed forces units was far below the authorized level. This condition was most apparent in senior command and staff positions and especially in the infantry battalions and armored cavalry squadrons. In 1969, for example, 47 percent of the infantry battalion commanders were two grades below authorization, and lieutenants and aspirants (officer candidates) were called upon to assume responsibilities beyond their experience or training. A major effort during the year centered on identifying and promoting qualified leaders. Yet, despite an increase of 2,653 senior officers between December 1968 and October 1969 (more promotions than in any other year), the regular Army still had only 63 percent of its authorized senior officers assigned. Rapid force expansion simply outpaced officer strength increases, and the armed forces supplemental August promotion board actions had little effect in raising the percentage of assigned senior officers. Additionally, most officers lacked formal training, although the amount of such training conducted at the Vietnamese armed forces leader-producing schools was slowly rising.

Another major headache which continued to plague both the regular and territorial forces was an imbalance of mid-level officers and noncommissioned officers grade structures. The situation stemmed mainly from what had been the inability of the Vietnamese armed forces officer and noncommissioned officer production and promotion systems to keep pace with the rapid mobilization. This problem was compounded by the fact that most of the officer and noncommissioned officer input had necessarily been at the bottom of their respective grade structures. The armed forces had no large pool of reserve officers or noncommissioned officers from which to draw; when some 1,055 reserve officers were recalled to active duty in early 1968, the pool was almost depleted. The armed forces developed a "three-year officer and NCO realization plan" which stipulated a progressive system of officer and noncommissioned officer promotions designed to achieve at least a 90 percent fill in all grades by the end of 1970. Owing in part to continued force structure increases, however, lack of eligible and qualified personnel for promotion and unrealistic promotion goals, all such projections proved too optimistic.

A third difficulty was the length of officer assignments. Some officers had never served away from the JGS headquarters, while others had stayed in combat units during their entire service. Military Assistance Command, Vietnam, initiated the development of a combined Personnel Systems Evaluation Committee to push a career management program, and the Joint General Staff finally adopted a limited officer rotation program which permitted officers who had served two years in one unit, upon request, to be reassigned to more desirable duties such as central agencies, schools, or the Joint General Staff. The policy was not fully implemented, however, and progress in the program was slow.

The most significant breakthrough in career management discipline was a plan for the progressive development of infantry officers. This plan was the Joint General Staff's first manpower management effort concerned with a particular category of personnel. It spelled out provisions for the career management of infantry officers, specified rotation of duty assignments between remote and more desirable areas, and included provisions for alternating tours between command and staff duty. Newly commissioned infantry officers were to serve their initial tours with combat units. Educational criteria for both military and civilian schools were prescribed for the selection of division, regimental, battalion, and sector commanders, for staff officers at all levels, and for service school cadres, to include the Command and Staff School. The program was basically similar to the U.S. Army's program for officer career management.

Efforts to remedy the grade structure by reforming the promotion system met with less success. No major renovation had occurred in the Vietnamese armed forces officer promotion system since 1965, but some reform took place in 1968 and 1969. Promotions were centralized within the Joint General Staff for all of the armed services, and a selection board was convened annually for all officer and noncommissioned officer grades. Even though well-defined, promotion goals were not met. In April 1970, Military Assistance Command published a comprehensive study of the system and recommended major changes, such as the establishment of separate promotion boards for the South Vietnam Navy and Air Force. The most serious problems and recommendations are noted below.

1. Too little credit was given for technical skill levels and qualifications in the promotion of the Vietnamese Air Force and Navy enlisted personnel. The basic eligibility criterion for their promotion was time in grade. Promotion considerations included nature of the units to which assigned, formal training, evaluation

by commanding officers, and awards for meritorious or valorous service. While all criteria were significant, none reflected the actual skill level and degree of qualification each soldier attained. The armed forces promotion system therefore did not ensure that the men who were promoted had the skills and qualifications required for their grade. This situation created difficulties in many technical areas. Personnel attaining senior noncommissioned officer status in the Vietnamese Navy or Air Force were frequently required to supervise the operation and care of sophisticated equipment or to be responsible for complex and important operations. If the senior noncommissioned officer lacked the skills required of his grade, the operational effectiveness of his unit was seriously reduced. Military Assistance Command recommended that grade-to-skill qualifications standards be developed, used as minimal prerequisites for promotion to E–4 and above, and the degree of qualification be given major weight in the promotion point system for the Navy and Air Force.

2. There were inconsistencies in the promotion system as it applied to the Women's Armed Forces Corps (WAFC) personnel. While WAFC personnel were supposed to be considered with all other Vietnamese armed forces personnel in the annual promotion selection, WAFC members in some instances were apparently considered, selected, and listed separately. Military Assistance Command recommended that all promotion selection boards be instructed to consider them at the same time and under the same criteria as other armed forces personnel, and that WAFC selectees be listed in the consolidated selection lists. This action would help provide fair promotion practices and would furnish correct promotion dates for WAFC selectees.

3. The manner in which the prerequisite for eligibility for promotion to major (a ninth grade level diploma required) was applied caused discontent. The requirement was designed to raise the educational level requirements for field grade officers without penalizing those field grade officers who had already achieved their rank without it (the diploma was not required for higher level promotion). Many officers believed this policy was an inequity in the system. Military Assistance Command recommended that the prerequisite be retained but that an explanation of its rationale be disseminated and provision made for educational level equivalency examinations for personnel desiring to qualify for major. Military Assistance Command also recommended that the Chief of Staff, Joint General Staff, be empowered to waive the educational requirement in exceptional cases.

4. There was a need to establish separate Regional Forces and

regular force battlefield promotions for noncommissioned officers and enlisted men. The existing system allocated quotas to each corps tactical zone, the Vietnamese Air Force, Navy, Special Forces, airborne, and Marine Corps. The four corps tactical zones and the Vietnamese Navy were allocated quotas which included Regional Forces personnel as well as regular force members. Results from 1969 showed that for the most part field commanders had not taken maximum advantage of battlefield promotion quotas; during the last six months, for example, only 32 percent of the total allocated quota for enlisted men had been used. By far the greater number of battlefield promotions went to the regular forces. To ensure fair and equitable treatment of Regional Forces personnel, it was recommended that two separate quotas be given to the designated commanders, one for the regular forces and one for the Regional Forces.

Vietnamese armed forces response to these recommendations was slow. In September 1971, the Joint General Staff amended the armed forces promotion policies and adjusted those parameters designed to recognize and accelerate promotions for able leaders; they also awarded extra promotion points to troops serving in combat and combat support units and reduced time in grade requirements for battlefield and nonbattlefield (meritorious) promotions. In consequence, the armed forces fulfilled its 1971 regular officer and noncommissioned officer promotion goals. However, sheer numbers and accelerated promotions alone did not necessarily ensure that the most effective leader was selected or that the overall leadership was upgraded. Moreover, despite significant emphasis on officer fill and promotions, commanders of maneuver battalions remained generally below authorized grades. The occupation was simply too dangerous and combat operations often eliminated the best commanders. In December 1970, 37 percent (forty-nine) of the infantry battalions were still commanded by captains. In January 1971, ninety-one of these officers were promoted to field rank, but increased combat operations and casualties took their toll. By 31 May, forty-six of the 133 infantry maneuver battalions (35 percent) were still commanded by captains; eighty of these 133 commanders had been in command one year or less, and fifty-two of those for less than six months.

Matériel

All these forces demanded vast quantities of military equipment, most of which was purchased or loaned from the United States. Deserving special attention were the efforts of General

Westmoreland and his successors to equip the Vietnamese infantry with modern small arms, communications, and transportation equipment. In 1964 the enemy had introduced the AK47, a modern, highly effective automatic rifle; later he began using a light but excellent series of rocket-propelled grenade (RPG) launchers against both armored and supply vehicles. In contrast, the South Vietnam forces were still armed with a variety of World War II weapons and, in view of the enemy's rising advantage in firepower, the MACV commander had asked that all South Vietnam Army ground combat units be equipped with the new U.S. lightweight M16 automatic rifle, as well as with other contemporary firearms. In the fall of 1965 he made an initial urgent request for 170,000 M16 rifles (later reduced to 100,000). But although the request was approved by the Joint Chiefs of Staff, Military Assistance Command was informed that U.S. forces in South Vietnam would receive first priority. After 1965 the increasing U.S. buildup slowly pushed Vietnamese armed forces matériel needs into the background. In December 1966 the Secretary of Defense directed that the issue of M16's to South Vietnam Army and Republic of Korea (ROK) forces be deferred and that the allocations previously planned for these forces be redirected to U.S. units. Finally, in March 1967, the allocation of M16 rifles for South Vietnamese and South Korean maneuver elements was reinstated, and the first shipments of rifles for the South Vietnam Army arrived the following month. But until 1968 there were only enough to equip the airborne and Marine battalions of the General Reserve.

In 1968 this situation began to change drastically. One new development was the end of the American buildup in South Vietnam and with it a leveling off of U.S. matériel demands. Two other developments were the decisions, first, in 1968 to support the more elaborate South Vietnamese armed forces structure outlined in the series of Improvement and Modernization programs and, second, in 1969 to Vietnamize the war by having the Vietnamese armed forces assume all American combat responsibilities. The result was a comprehensive logistical effort to supply the South Vietnamese military forces with superior small arms as quickly as possible. By mid-1968 all of the South Vietnamese Army infantry battalions had received the new weapons, along with other contemporary small arms—the new U.S. M60 machine gun, the M79 grenade launcher, and the LAW (or light antitank weapon). In the years that followed, South Vietnamese Army combat support units, the territorial forces, and the Civilian Irregular Defense Group received identical equipment. Together, these small arms gave a significant morale and psychological boost to the South Vietnamese soldier by allowing him to meet the enemy with equal or greater firepower. The standardization of small arms also simplified the equally important matters of logistics and maintenance.

Before 1968 the South Vietnamese Army also had severe shortages in crew-served weapons, tactical communications equipment, and light transport vehicles, items that were critical to an Army composed mostly of foot soldiers. To overcome these deficiencies, Military Assistance Command instituted temporary loan procedures whereby the Vietnamese armed forces highest priority requirements were met by temporary transfers from U.S. depots and excess stocks. By md-1968, equipment valued at approximately $10 million was on loan to the Vietnamese Army and included 691 $\frac{1}{4}$-ton trucks, 388 $2\frac{1}{2}$-ton trucks, 151 $\frac{1}{4}$-ton trailers, 208 106-mm. recoilless rifles, 100 M60 machine gun mounts, 4,932 .50-caliber machine gun mounts, 18 .50-caliber machine guns, and 177 survey sets. Once the Improvement and Modernization programs began to take effect in 1969, however, this practice stopped and the Vietnamese armed forces shortages in these areas were rapidly made up.

After 1969 most armed forces matériel needs were satisfied from existing U.S. stocks in South Vietnam. As U.S. units redeployed, most of their equipment and supplies were turned in, reconditioned, if necessary, by U.S. logistical units, and reissued to the Vietnamese armed forces units as appropriate. Requirements that could not be satisfied in this manner were met from the Pacific Command supply and maintenance facilities or shipped from CONUS sources. This practice was expanded by the Vietnamization Logistics Program which began in July 1971. Major objectives of the new program were the acceleration of equipment deliveries and the expansion of Vietnamese armed forces secondary item stockage.

Project ENHANCE in May 1972 began to augment the armed forces capabilities as one response to the North Vietnamese Army offensive in April. The purpose of the project was to accelerate the delivery of the residual balance of fiscal year 1972 and 1973 Phase III assets, replace all abnormal armed forces combat losses projected through the end of fiscal year 1972, and provide the armed forces with selected agumentation capabilities. Initially, Project ENHANCE required that large quantities of matériel be delivered to the Vietnamese armed forces as soon as possible. To avoid overburdening the armed forces with matériel that it was ili-prepared to absorb, utilize, or maintain, execution of the program was relaxed to the extent that the MACV commander was authorized to call forward quantities of matériel that would on

MAINTENANCE CLASSES FOR NEW EQUIPMENT

arrival immediately support or "enhance" the Vietnamese armed forces capabilities. This shift to a "pull" versus "push" concept in no way de-emphasized the high priority assigned to the project. But the flexibility provided by relaxation of the required delivery dates enabled Military Assistance Command to run the program more efficiently. These efforts were continued until the implementation of the cease-fire accords early in 1973.

As the variety of equipment and supplies given to the Vietnamese armed forces grew, it became a more "balanced" and thus a more specialized institution. Once the number of infantry units became stabilized, the various combat controlling headquarters were then slowly filled out with engineer, signal, ordnance, and logistical support units. The rising number of artillery battalions (from twenty-nine in June 1968 to fifty-eight by 1972) and armored cavalry squadrons (from eleven to seventeen) has already been noted. New elements in the Vietnamese Army inventory were Rome Plows for land-clearing, 175-mm. artillery pieces on the demilitarized zone (South Vietnam's border with North Vietnam), and, in the fall of 1971, the first battalion of M48 medium battle tanks. It may be added that, although beyond the scope of this work, the expansion of the Vietnamese Navy and Air Force—both technical services—was also highlighted by the acquisition of what was for the Vietnamese extremely sophisticated equipment.

Training Overview

The technical expansion of the South Vietnam armed forces placed great demands on the schools and training centers. Military

Assistance Command continuously sought to maintain and improve these institutions so that the Vietnamese forces would be more than an army on paper. New schools and training centers were established and existing facilities improved and expanded to upgrade their training capacity. Course content was constantly reviewed and revised to ensure it was meeting field requirements; Military Assistance Command continued to pay special attention to leadership training, small unit and night operations, marksmanship training, and ambush and patrol tactics. New courses of instruction, such as the special officer candidate, company commander, regional forces officer refresher, and methods of instruction, were established in all schools. At Regional Forces and Popular Forces training centers, consolidation programs were initiated in order to improve training facilities and standardize and upgrade training activities. Finally, MAC started programs to improve the leadership and cadre in the Vietnamese Army training base, and made vigorous efforts to place combat-experienced soldiers throughout these centers.

During 1968 the expansion and improvement of the training base enabled the South Vietnam Army to meet all of their training requirements. Service school inputs rose from 53,000 students in 1967 to 70,000 by the end of the year. The volume handled by the training centers was much larger and included some 168,335 Vietnamese Army and Regional Forces recruits, 19,174 OCS preparatory course students, 22,483 Popular Forces recruits, 13 new and 13 old infantry battalions (refresher training), 44 new Regional Forces heavy weapons platoons, 588 new Popular Forces platoons, and refresher training for 656 old Popular Forces platoons. With enemy activity low and mobilization efforts successful, this pace continued throughout the following years.

From 1968 to 1970 U.S. attempts to develop the size and scope of the training base also met with success. The service school system grew to a total of twenty-six schools offering training in 326 different courses of instruction with a normal capacity of 24,000 students expandable to an emergency capacity of 34,000. Training centers, including Regional and Popular Forces, Ranger, and the ten division training centers, numbered thirty-three and were located throughout the country. These centers provided instruction in a total of thirty-four different courses and had a normal capacity of approximately 65,000 students, with an emergency capacity of about 105,655. Formal training needs which could not be satisfied within the Vietnamese armed forces system—pilots and operators of complex signal equipment for example—continued to be met by CONUS installations or by special U.S. service mobile training teams in South Vietnam. Hereafter the emphasis would be on quality rather than quantity.

In January 1970 the Chief of Staff, U.S. Army, dispatched a special DA training team to South Vietnam headed by Brigadier General Donnelly P. Bolton for the purpose of examining the state of U.S. training advice. A month later the team recommended several measures to strengthen the American training advisory system. Most important was the matter of personnel, and in the following months the Department of the Army gave much attention to both the quantity and the quality of the replacements it was sending to the MACV Training Directorate. By September 1970 the assigned strength of the MACV training advisory element rose from 55 to over 100 percent, and by June 1971 over 90 percent of the training advisers were combat experienced. At the end of the year the training advisory element numbered over 3,500, but thereafter it decreased until the total withdrawal in March 1973. Other major accomplishments with DA encouragement during this period were the publication of a five-year Vietnamese armed forces training program and training budget in 1971, the revision of all armed forces training programs of instruction (over 650), and the institution of a "sister service school system" whereby similar U.S. and Vietnamese Army schools maintained liaison on a regular basis. Finally, the practice of Central Training Command (CTC) level refresher training was ended and instead divisions instituted their own annual training programs assisted, when necessary, by mobile training teams from the Training Command.

School and Training Center Improvements

In April 1971 the Joint General Staff conducted an appraisal of all instructor positions to determine which required combat-experienced personnel, and on the basis of its findings directed certain reallocations. The number of positions was reduced from 1,685 to 710, and the criteria for the replacement of long-tenure officers in key training center and service school positions were strengthened and enforced. As a result, 138 combat-experienced instructors were added during the year in areas dealing with command, operations, tactics, and weapons. Recognizing that combat experience alone did not guarantee a good instructor, the Central Training Command introduced a six-week method of instruction course in June at the Quang Trung Training Center. In addition, a one-week method of instruction refresher course was established at the remaining training centers and in thirteen of the twenty-three service schools. The appointment of combat-experienced senior commanders to the key Vietnamese armed forces training installations added strength and validity to the training program. (*Map 2*)

In June 1971 Military Assistance Command began a series of briefings designed to acquaint the faculties of the Vietnamese armed forces training centers and service schools with a proposed Training Management System. The key element in the proposal was a systematic approach to curriculum development called Instructional System Development (ISD). In essence Instructional System Development was an eight-step model for the development of a course of instruction. The Central Training Command favored the proposal, and on 27 July Military Assistance Command presented a new two-week curriculum development and management course to selected members of the CTC staff. Subsequently, Military Assistance Command prepared twenty-one related draft directives and manuals for the Central Training Command; these training materials were essential for the proper implementation of the Training Management System and Instructional System Development within the armed forces. The first of eight calendar year 1971 classes in August began teaching staff officers and training managers of the service schools and training centers the fundamentals of ISD techniques.

By 13 January 1972, eight classes had been completed and 102 officers had graduated. The Central Training Command put together a workable Vietnamese version of Instructional System Development and, in co-ordination with U.S. advisers, supervised the system engineering of a pilot program at the Vietnamese armed forces ordnance school. The goals for the immediate future were to complete the instructor training so that CTC officers could take over the presentation of the curriculum development and management course and conduct the first ISD course entirely in the Vietnamese language.

A consolidation of the training centers began in 1970 as a measure to increase training center capacity at the lowest possible cost. Military Assistance Command was vitally concerned with the facilities to upgrade water system improvement programs connected with this consolidation and also with those improvements planned for service schools. The 1970–71 Military Assistance Service Funded Military Construction (MASF/MILCON) Program apportioned $28 million for these projects. A total of twenty-three national, Regional Forces, Popular Forces, and Ranger training centers were to be improved, modernized, consolidated into ten "national" centers by the end of 1972. The consolidation plan

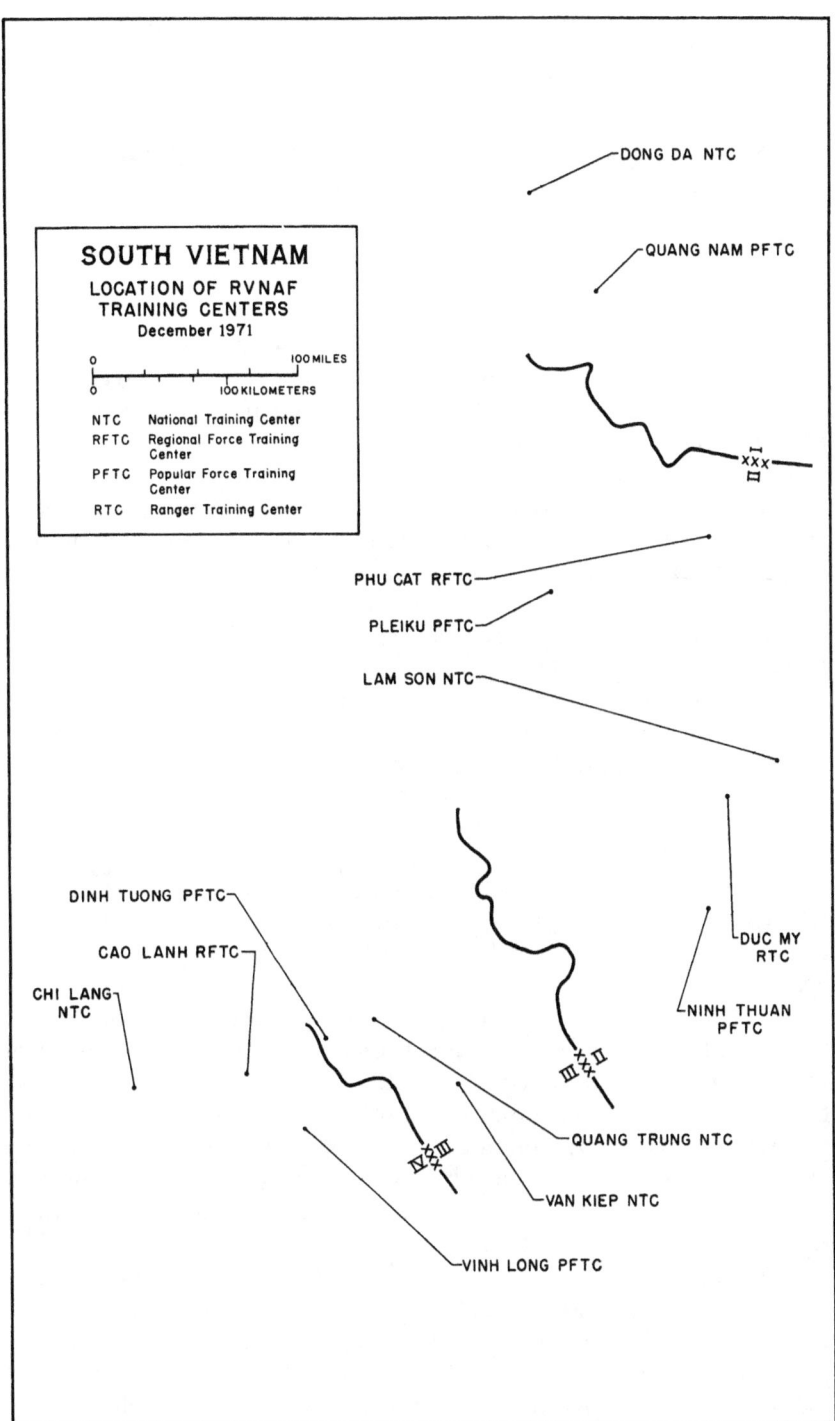

MAP 2

proceeded on schedule and five Popular Forces training centers were closed by the end of the first quarter, 1971.

During the second quarter of 1971, the completion date for consolidation was accelerated owing to increased Cambodian training requirements, an accelerated construction program, and the additional training commitments generated by the 357 new Popular Forces platoons which had been formed in IV Corps Tactical Zone. At the end of December the consolidation program was 92 percent complete. Three Popular Forces training centers remained active after their designated training termination date; however, these centers were scheduled to end all training during the first two weeks of January 1972, and the entire program was targeted for completion on 31 January. By then, thirteen underutilized centers had been closed down and the more efficient "National Training Center" system instituted.

In 1971, for the first time, the Central Training Command adopted a selected graduation system for Vietnamese noncommissioned officer and specialist training programs. This move reflected the increased interest in quality, and contrasted with the past policy of graduating every student who "completed" the course. One by-product of this change was the establishment of slow-learner, remedial training courses and various make-up training programs, all of which were new practices for the Vietnamese armed forces.

A facilities upgrade plan for the centers was designed to complement the consolidation program. Minimum additional facilities were to be constructed to accommodate increased training loads, existing facilities were to be rehabilitated, and water supply and distillation systems were to be installed. By the end of December the training center upgrade program was 92 percent complete with total completion expected by the end of the third quarter of fiscal year 1972.

The MASF/MILCON projects for the service school totaled $9,319,000. The facility upgrade projects ($7,845,000) consisted of rehabilitation and new construction of barracks, classrooms, mess halls, kitchen, latrines, ranges, and other buildings. Water upgrade projects ($1,474,000) included drilling additional wells, laying water distribution lines, building water storage areas, and providing necessary water pumps. By 31 March 1971 all facility and water upgrade projects were under way.

During March the MACV/MASF Military Construction Review Board approved a project for construction of a Vietnamese infantry school at Bearcat Camp (III Corps Tactical Zone) at a projected cost of $7 million. Because of funding restrictions and higher priority projects, this decision temporarily canceled a previous plan to form a combined arms school at Bearcat and construct new armor and infantry schools there.

By August, eight of the twenty-two facilities upgrade projects were completed as were fifteen of the eighteen water projects; blueprints for the Bearcat Infantry School had been completed, contract negotiations were in progress, and the notice to proceed was received in November 1971. When 1971 ended the $28 million construction program for twenty-seven installations was 96 percent complete in dollar value; twenty-two of the twenty-seven projects were finished and the remaining five were programed for completion by the spring of 1972.

Combined Arms Training

In June 1971, with the reduction of both U.S. conventional and advisory forces, a question arose regarding the Vietnamese armed forces capability to employ air support and effectively direct air-ground operations. The high-intensity combat operations in Laos and Cambodia made it evident that the armed forces staffs needed strengthening in planning and co-ordinating fire support, airmobile operations, and logistical support. To ensure that this goal received proper command emphasis, in August 1971 the MACV commander admonished his U.S. advisers to urge their counterparts to conduct command post exercises and war games which would include exercises in multiregiment operations at corps level and multibattalion operations at regiment level. Concurrently, the MACV commander recommended that the chief of the Joint General Staff direct his corps commanders to place command and staff emphasis on measures to strengthen battlefield reporting procedures.

In late August a joint combined committee was approved by the chief of the Joint General Staff and formed under the supervision of the Central Training Command to develop a combined arms doctrine suitable for the Vietnam environment. Also in August the Vietnamese armor school conducted eight hours of combined arms training for four airborne battalions, marking for all service schools the start of a program to increase the effectiveness of combined arms operations.

Throughout September the joint committee devoted itself to the development of a Combined Arms Doctrinal Manual, the first effort by the Vietnamese to produce a formal doctrine. The proposed draft, suitable for armed forces application on the battlefield and for use as a training guide, was reviewed by Chief, Central Training Command, and approved by Chief, Joint General Staff, in November. In advance of the document's publication, the Commander, U.S. Military Assistance Command, Vietnam, advised field elements that the doctrine was forthcoming and that ". . . proper meshing of air, artillery, naval gunfire, infantry, and armor in accordance with the new doctrine will do much to enhance RVNAF supremacy over the NVA/VC. Advisors and commanders of each US service [are] expected to give dynamic support to the early introduction of this new mode of tactics on the Southeast Asia battlefield."

Distributed January 1972, the new combined arms handbook represented a milestone in the Vietnamese armed forces progress and effectiveness. The new tactical approach was first applied by the Vietnamese Airborne Division in mid-December 1971 during its push through Krek to the Chup Rubber Plantation. The results were favorable and the division and corps commanders indicated firm acceptance of the new doctrine. Since the cease-fire, with the inactivation of the separate armor and infantry schools, and the consolidation of these schools at the new Bearcat Combined Arms Center, the Vietnamese armed forces continued to emphasize this approach.

Middle Management Training

To develop and train Vietnamese armed forces middle management assets, Military Assistance Command tasked the Advanced Research Projects Agency (ARPA), Office of the Secretary of Defense, with instituting a specialized training program for key management personnel in communications and selected support areas. On 15 December 1970, a one-year contract was awarded to Booz-Allen Applied Research, Inc., to implement the ARPA program and develop the Middle Management Training (MMT) Program for selected officer groups in the Vietnamese armed forces. Advanced courses were to be developed as follow-on training to the existing armed forces basic management training course, Program Review and Analysis Improvement Systems Evaluation, taught at the Vietnamese Logistics Management School. The program was to be documented to serve as a prototype for future training programs in Vietnam or other areas with a similar culture, and from the outset plans had been made to turn the project over to the Vietnamese armed forces as part of Vietnamization.

The specific technical fields selected for the pilot program were supply and maintenance, transportation, and communications-electronics. On 4 March 1971, Booz-Allen briefed Military Assistance Command and Major General Phan Trong Chinh, Chief, Central Training Command, on the scope, general content, and schedule of the program. The advanced courses were to run for seven weeks, presented in three cycles, two in English and the third in Vietnamese. General Chinh approved the plan and the first course, in communications, began 21 June 1971.

The first supply and management course given at the Vietnamese Logistic Management School and the first transportation course at the transportation school began on 5 July 1971, each with twenty students. The first communications-electronic MMT class graduated 9 August 1971. The supply maintenance and logistics MMT classes were completed 21 August 1971. The remaining two classes for each course graduated on 11 December 1971, after which the program became a Vietnamese responsibility.

Advanced Technical Training

In 1971 progress was also indicated in the development of the technically sophisticated and applied production skills. The first class in advanced engineering (twenty-eight students) began at the Military Technical Engineering School, Saigon, on 7 August 1971. This school had a staff of contract university professors and would produce many times more graduate engineers than all of the civilian universities in Vietnam. The engineering course included such vital skills as advance construction, public works, and road and bridge construction.

On 6 September the Vietnamese armed forces opened a school for bridge design. Each class had a maximum capacity of fourteen students who were required to design and supervise the actual construction of a bridge as part of the curriculum. Graduates were highly valued by a country whose waterways and water crossings play a very key role in its economy.

The armed forces ability to operate sophisticated equipment was exemplified by its success in the Integrated Communications System (ICS). The communications system required trained personnel in the fields of microwave, tropospheric scatter radio, fixed plant carriers, and the countrywide dial telephone system. Training in support of this system was conducted in South Vietnam and in the United States. In Vietnam, U.S. civilian contract instructors taught basic, intermediate, and advanced electronics to operators of the system; in the United States, Vietnamese armed forces students received special training as fixed station technical controllers, dial central office repairmen, and communications traffic managers.

On 3 February 1971, the first class of eleven microwave repairmen graduated from the ICS training facility located at the Vietnamese armed forces signal school in Vung Tau. Between February

BRIDGE CONSTRUCTION TRAINING, ENGINEER SCHOOL

and December additional communications instruction was progressively transferred to the Vietnamese signal school from the U.S. Crypto–Log Support Center, Saigon, the Vietnamese 60th Signal Depot, Saigon, and the U.S. 1st Signal Brigade at Long Binh.

The first class of the dial control repair course graduated at Vung Tau on 16 March 1971. In August the first group of third echelon cryptographic repairmen completed training, and in September the fourth echelon radar and switchboard repair courses were transferred to Vung Tau. By December the fourth and fifth echelon teletypewriter repair course and the fourth echelon signal repair courses were also being conducted at the Vietnamese signal school. The majority of courses were still being conducted by U.S. civilians at the end of December, but the target date for the Vietnamese armed forces to assume the entire ICS mission was 1 November 1972.

Pilot Training for the South Vietnam Air Force

Once U.S. redeployment began in earnest, the training and

STUDENTS AT VUNG TAU SIGNAL SCHOOL

buildup of the South Vietnam Air Force also took on a new importance. While the Army retained jurisdiction over helicopters within its sphere, in the South Vietnam government defense organization these critical machines were controlled by the Air Force. Thus, after 1969 the rapid buildup of the Air Force's rotary-wing arm necessitated close co-ordination between CONUS training schedules, U.S. Army aviation redeployments, equipment turnover procedures, and U.S. Air Force advisory teams. In many cases Vietnamese Air Force pilots and mechanics served long apprentice periods with Army aviation companies before their own squadrons were finally activated. Again the result was impressive. In 1968 the Air Force possessed about seventy–five outmoded rotary aircraft (H–34's) organized into five squadrons; by the end of 1972 it boasted some 500 new machines in eighteen squadrons, one of the largest, costliest, and most modern helicopter fleets in the world.

Both U.S. Army and U.S. Air Force CONUS installations were used extensively to train Vietnamese Air Force pilots. This practice made it necessary for all prospective pilots to receive extensive language training. English language training for all Vietnamese

VIETNAMESE STUDENT PILOTS, FT. STEWART, GA.

helicopter pilots was finally completed on schedule with the last group leaving for the United States in April 1971. CONUS helicopter pilot training was scheduled for completion in July 1972. At the time, a total of 1,642 would have been trained including 341 who would have received instrument qualification training.

The total Vietnamese Air Force offshore pilot training requirement, including helicopter, fixed-wing, and high-performance aircraft, was 3,334. During 1971, 1,007 students departed for offshore training while the remainder were scheduled to depart for continental United States by May 1972 for eighteen months of training. Completion date for the major portion of the offshore pilot program was September 1973.

On-the-Job Training

Another effort which provided excellent experience for the South Vietnam Army was the on-the-job training program, actually a series of programs. It began in 1968 in response to current Vietnamization planning and the new equipment being made available

SIGNAL TRAINING FOR VIETNAMESE, *sponsored by 1st Signal Brigade.*

under the Improvement and Modernization plans. In many cases, both Vietnamese Army users and instructors lacked the ability to handle the more complex equipment. To overcome this handicap, the 1st Logistical Command began Operation BUDDY, under the direction of Major General Joseph M. Heiser, Jr. BUDDY was a large on-the-job training effort using American expertise and equipment in the 1st Logistical Command to train Vietnamese personnel. In general, U.S. logistical units adopted similar Vietnamese Army units and conducted a variety of programs to enhance their effectiveness, such as integrated operations, training courses, and occasional social events where members could become familiar with each others activities and problems. The U.S. engineer and signal commands initiated similar efforts. In addition, U.S. logistical services also supervised a number of SWITCHBACK operations, whereby a deploying U.S. unit turned over its equipment directly to a newly activated Vietnamese Army unit of the same type. Both practices proved successful in speeding up the Vietnamese armed forces Improvement and Modernization programs, and showed that U.S. service support units were capable of accomplishing extensive training and advisory tasks in addition to their primary, functional missions.

In most cases, on-the-job training programs were decentralized and were developed on the initiative of local commanders. Later, in 1970, they became more formalized in order to handle the larger volume of combat support and combat service support unit activations. These programs varied in length from a few days to several months to over a year and included instruction for both regular and territorial officers and enlisted personnel. The objectives of the programs varied in scope from improving an individual's existing skills to giving him an entirely new capability. Normally on-the-job training was used to acquire and refine highly complex technical skills, especially the repair and maintenance of electronic equipment and machinery. Personnel in on-the-job training fell into four broad categories:

1. trainees detailed to commute and report on a scheduled basis to a U.S. unit for on-the-job training;

2. trainees attached full time to U.S. units for a specified period of training and, upon completion of the on-the-job training cycle, returned to Vietnamese units for proper skill utilization;

3. trainees attached to U.S. units for a specified period of training and, upon completion of the on-the-job training cycle, assigned to positions in the same or a similar unit, replacing U.S. personnel (more trainees would then be attached for on-the-job training, and this sequence would continue until sufficient men were trained to allow the South Vietnamese to assume complete responsibility for the mission; a new Vietnamese unit might officially be activated later); and

4. Vietnamese personnel trained on the job in their present units by U.S. mobile training teams and, upon completion of this training, utilized within their current unit.

Experience showed that the most effective on-the-job training efforts were in the mechanical fields where students learned by watching and imitating. Effectiveness diminished in programs which required a knowledge of theory and related applications. The expansion potential of the on-the-job training programs was thus restricted only by the inability of trainees with limited qualifications to handle complex modern equipment. The language barrier was the second major problem. In many instances, the Vietnamese language equivalent for certain technical terms was too different to use without sacrificing a great deal of precision and understanding.

Combined Operations

For nontechnical combat skills, combined and joint operations between Vietnamese and U.S. units constituted a special type of on-the-job training. In theory, by operating with American units, Vietnamese forces would acquire valuable practical experience that could not be duplicated in formal training. Before 1968, the largest organized effort of this sort was the Combined Action Program run by the III Marine Amphibious Force in the northern quarter of South Vietnam. Marine rifle squads were married with Popular Forces platoons defending countryside hamlets; the two units worked together for several months until local security had improved to the degree that the marine were no longer needed. The program achieved success at the local level, but was too costly in terms of manpower to apply to the entire country.

U.S. Army units had conducted similar types of effort since 1965, but had been unable to pursue them in systematic fashion owing to the pressure of combat operations. The first large-scale effort occurred late in 1966 when U.S. and Vietnamese infantry battalions were paired and tasked to support pacification efforts in three key districts close to Saigon in Gia Dinh Province. The endeavor, Operation FAIRFAX, was pushed by General Westmoreland who hoped that the three participating U.S. battalions would inspire the Vietnamese Army and territorial units involved. The U.S. battalions came from three different U.S. infantry divisions and were thus able to channel considerable U.S. combat support resources into the operation. In theory, however, all units—the U.S. and Vietnamese Army infantry battalions and the territorial and paramilitary forces under district (subsector) control—were to act in concert through co-operation and mutual respect.

Initially the program was beset by co-ordination and control difficulties; minor problems sometimes became major issues in the absence of higher command direction. Successful combined operations were demonstrated the following year in Gia Dinh Province, when a Vietnamese Ranger group headquarters and the 199th Light Infantry Brigade, commanded by Brigadier General John F. Freund, assumed responsibility for the direction of the multicomponent effort. Finally in November 1967, the 199th Brigade was withdrawn leaving only Ranger and province forces in charge, an early example of Vietnamization.

After *Tet* 1968 these types of operations become more common. As a rule, Vietnamese units remained under Vietnamese commanders except in a few cases where U.S. and Vietnamese units exchanged or "cross-attached" small tactical units (platoons or squads) with one another. In I Corps Tactical Zone, III Marine Amphibious Force continued its successful Combined Action Program effort while Lieutenant General Richard G. Stilwell, the new XXIV Corps commander, went further and began integrating all U.S. and Vietnamese Army tactical operations in his area of responsibility. Under his direction, all multibattalion operations were conducted with a mix of U.S. and Vietnamese battalions acting in concert, but not under a unified command. Operations were conceived jointly by General Stilwell and Major General Truong, commanding general of the 1st Vietnamese Army Division, and each contributed a share of the forces against common objectives. During these combined efforts, U.S. brigade and Vietnamese regimental commanders often established neighboring command posts in the same fire support bases and conducted operations through close and continuous co-operation. Stilwell and Truong worked closely together and spent most of their days in the same helicopter alternately visiting U.S. and Vietnamese units. The psychological and practical effect of these visits brought about a complete integration of military effort and a high degree of co-operation between the Vietnamese and American forces. The resulting partnership initially made possible some tutelage by U.S. commanders at battalion and brigade levels for their Vietnamese counterparts; later, there was a little "reverse lend-lease" in this arrangement as the seasoned Vietnamese commanders were able to pass on their experience to newly arrived U.S. leaders.

This practice was fully supported by Major General Melvin Zais as commanding general of the U.S. 101st Airborne Division, and subsequently as Stilwell's successor in 1969–70, when he pushed similar methods in the 1st Marine and the Americal Divisions. Actually, the Americal Division was well along with its combined operations program under Major General Lloyd B. Ramsey and the vast improvement in the 2d Vietnamese Army Division's performance dates from this period. The Americal Division established common brigade-regimental tactical areas for which the U.S. and Vietnamese units were jointly responsible; in each area U.S. brigades and Vietnamese regiments collocated their command posts at the same base camps and conducted extensive combined operations. In II Corps Tactical Zone, combined operations programs were begun by Lieutenant General William R. Peers in early 1968. While the 4th Infantry Division guarded the highland approaches, Peers started a "Pair-Off" program between units of the 173d Airborne Brigade and the Vietnamese 22d and 23d Infantry Divisions. Later the concept was expanded to include Vietnamese artillery and other combat support forces, especially newly established units. In

1969 and 1970 these same Vietnamese units replaced American forces, as they deployed from South Vietnam, almost on a unit-for-unit basis.

Similar efforts were initiated later in III Corps Tactical Zone by Lieutenant General Julian J. Ewell, commanding the II Field Force, Vietnam. In mid-1969 Ewell began a corps-wide Dong Tien or "Progress Together" program that paired the 1st and 25th U.S. Infantry Divisions and the 199th Light Infantry Brigade with three Vietnamese infantry divisions. Combined operations were most extensive between the 1st U.S. and 5th Vietnamese Infantry Divisions and paved the way for the 5th Division's assumption of almost all of the Big Red One's area of operation the following year. Finally, on the border areas of III Corps Tactical Zone, II Field Force mated Vietnamese airborne regiments with brigades of the 1st Cavalry Division (Airmobile); there the airborne units made extensive use of the American division's large helicopter resources and became proficient in the more sophisticated methods used by U.S. units. In retrospect, the Dong Tien effort served as an invaluable training prelude to the Cambodian invasion in April 1970 during which the Vietnamese III Corps Tactical Zone headquarters put three brigade-size task forces on the road to Phom Penh with minimal American assistance. As in other corps tactical zones, such programs not only served as training vehicles, but they also provided a transitional period during which Vietnamese commanders could gradually ease into their new responsibilities as the U.S. forces departed.

Mobile Advisory Teams

With the exception of the Combined Action Program and a few other programs, neither on-the-job training nor the combined operations programs had any effect on the territorial units. Yet, as U.S. forces deployed from South Vietnam and were replaced by Vietnamese regular units, the ability of the Regional and Popular Forces to provide security for pacification became more critical. Up to 1968 the territorial forces had been without advisers, and often Military Assistance Command had little information on their condition and employment. With thousands of these units spread out over the country any effort to place permanent advisers with them would have been too costly in terms of U.S. manpower. In an effort to begin improving them, General Westmoreland was at first forced to rely heavily on the initiative of the corps senior advisers and the U.S. resources available within each corps tactical zone. In 1967 all U.S. corps headquarters initiated Regional and Popular Forces training programs utilizing mobile training teams composed of from three to ten members who rotated among local Regional and Popular units. Their mission varied from conducting one-day on-site training to five-week refresher training programs. The teams were given a number of military labels—combined mobile training teams, combined mobile improvement teams, "red-catcher" and "impact" teams, and Regional Forces company training teams. However, these efforts proved too decentralized and unco-ordinated to deal with what was an extremely difficult problem.

Encouraged by the limited progress that had been made, General Westmoreland directed a countrywide test of the Regional Forces company training team concept. Basically, the concept was similar to the Marine Combined Action Program. In practice, a team of three company grade officers and three noncommissioned officers joined a Regional Forces company at a Vietnamese Army training center, assisted in training, and then accompanied the unit back to its home base for in-place training and operational missions. The team remained until the unit was capable of operating alone, usually six to nine months later. The team did not command the unit, but Regional Forces commanders were instructed to follow the team's directions. The Regional Forces company training team was in the business of training and supervising, not simply advising, and thus had a more active role than that of the advisory teams. Team members were recognized combat leaders with about nine months left in the country and some command of the Vietnamese language. By the end of 1967, advisor reports did not reflect any significant improvement in the territorial forces. However, there was general agreement that the training team concept was valid and should be expanded. At a conference held on 26 October 1967, General Westmoreland recommended that some 354 new advisory teams be created specifically to provide assistance to the Regional and Popular Forces. Other recommendations called for providing engineer and personnel advisers to each of the forty-four provinces. What finally evolved were the mobile advisory team and the mobile advisory logistics team. These teams formed the nucleus of a massive improvement program that addressed all aspects of the administration, logistical support, and tactical operations of the territorial units.

Each mobile advisory team consisted of two officers, three enlisted men, and a Vietnamese Army interpreter. Their primary mission was to advise and instruct Regional Forces companies and Popular Forces platoons and Regional and Popular Forces group headquarters on field fortifications, barrier systems, indirect fire support, and small unit operations with emphasis on night operations and ambushes, patrols, weapons employment, emergency

MAT Adviser Examines Homemade PF Mortar

medical care, and other topics related to Regional and Popular Forces missions. By the end of 1968 the MACV deployment goal had been met and the program was judged a success.

Two significant changes were later made in the program centering around personnel procurement. Initially, personnel were drawn from individuals in U.S. units who still had at least six months remaining in Vietnam. In early 1969, however, mobile advisory team members were assigned directly from the CONUS personnel stream to a specific mobile advisory team for a one-year tour. Tour stability was important and advisers could often pick up more experience in one or two months in their advisory capacity than by serving six with a U.S. unit. In order to be better prepared for the assignment, advisers attended a new adviser school established by the U.S. Army, Vietnam (USARV), at Di An. In order to make mobile advisory team duty more desirable, the second change stipulated that the mobile advisory team leader and his assistant would receive command credit for their duty.

The mobile advisory team concept was hailed as the turning point in improving the effectiveness of the territorial forces, and the program was continually strengthened during the years that followed. The detailed structure changed from time to time, but in general the teams remained small, close-knit groups with new company grade officers, a light weapons noncommissioned officer, a radiotelephone operator, and an interpreter. Although the mobile advisory teams initially concentrated on working with Regional Forces companies, later they operated with the smaller Popular Forces platoons, and in the end they became extensions of first the province and then the district advisory teams. The mobile advisory teams remained mobile, however, and were transferred to other areas whenever necessary. Since 1970 the mobile advisory teams' success has been periodically reflected in the fine performance shown by territorial units operating independently and with minimal outside support.

The mobile advisory logistics team progam complemented the mobile advisory team and placed major emphasis on improving the administrative and logistic support procedures of the Regional and Popular Forces. The mobile advisory logistics teams' missions were to provide on-the-spot administrative, supply, and logistics training and assistance to Regional and Popular Forces units and their direct support logistical companies and depots. As was the case with the mobile advisory teams, initial personnel resources were detailed from USARV resources and later replacements were obtained through normal MACV channels. The mobile advisory logistics teams proved to be an effective means of improving the administrative and logistical functions of the territorial forces and contributed to their high morale and increased matériel independence. No longer were they the forgotten stepchildren of the Republic of Vietnam armed forces.

How successful were U.S. efforts to improve the effectiveness of the South Vietnamese Army during these final years of U.S. involvement? The test came during North Vietnam's spring offensive of 1972. The commendable performance on the part of the South Vietnamese Army and the territorial forces was ample evidence that U.S. effort had not failed. The Vietnamese Army withstood and repelled the vicious onslaught of the enemy, and its success instilled a new sense of esprit and national unity throughout the country. The policy of Vietnamization had not only made it possible for U.S. military forces to disengage from South Vietnam, but it also helped to create a South Vietnamese Army strong enough to take their place.

CHAPTER V

Overview

General

Although overshadowed by the more dramatic actions on the battlefields of Vietnam, the U.S. training mission has been one of the most critical aspects of U.S. involvement in Southeast Asia. From the beginning in 1954, the U.S. mission was to "advise and assist" the government of Vietnam in training a military force capable of defending the nation. Some of the more important facets of this task have been the establishment, development, consolidation, improvement, and support of military service schools and training centers, the development of programs of instruction, and assistance in evaluating and planning requirements and capabilities. Although many obstacles were never completely overcome, U.S. accomplishment in the area of training have been impressive in light of the expansion of the Vietnamese armed forces from a U.S. supported force of 150,000 in 1956 to its subsequent authorized strength of over one million. In the following pages an attempt will be made to summarize these accomplishments and at the same time to present some of the more serious recurring headaches that beset the training effort.

Training Centers

The Vietnamese armed forces school training system expanded from one national training center in 1956 to a total of thirty-three by 1970. This rapid growth was necessary in view of the qualitative and quantitative expansion of the military forces. In an effort to improve training, U.S. advisory teams were assigned to each training center on an almost continual basis. However, headway in this area was generally extremely slow.

The most significant obstacle to effective training was poor leadership at the training center level. The most highly qualified officers should have been placed in training positions; but too often these posts were filled by officers who were relieved of combat commands. Their superiors often reasoned that such officers could do less damage in these positions of seemingly little responsibility than as combat officers and, in the short run, their logic was probably sound. But poor leadership at the top quickly affected lower echelons, starting a cycle of poor training and poor combat effectiveness. Although advisers have long noted this deficiency, the Vietnamese have been reluctant to relieve incompetent center commanders, possibly because they lacked suitable replacements.

The low quality of cadre personnel also impeded the training mission. By and large, most cadres were not sufficiently knowledgeable in their subject areas and members lacked any real motivation to develop from a trainee into a combat-ready soldier. Perpetuating the inefficient cadre corps was the tradition of "homesteading" cadre personnel for up to five years. Such inbreeding only worsened a bad situation. Ideas became stagnant and progress merely trickled along; modern techniques and doctrine developed and practiced each day by combat units, unless inculcated by the advisers, often failed to reach the student, and often even the advisers were unaware of current tactics and techniques. The job of providing combat-experienced cadres received much emphasis, and a program was instituted to replace instructors without recent combat experience with people fresh from combat units. But this policy was not entirely successful because field commanders, when levied to support the program, often kept their best men and sent only marginal personnel. Not surprising, many of the replacements lacked the aptitude and motivation for cadre duty, and the duty itself suffered a corresponding lack of prestige.

Most of the other deficiencies within the training centers were by-products of the leadership and cadre difficulties. Instructional techniques were poor: instruction was presented almost entirely through the lecture method with little emphasis on practical work or demonstrations. A strong disregard prevailed for the use of concurrent or integrated training techniques. Instructors appeared to look upon lesson plans as something to be covered as quickly as possible with no regard for their obligation to impart knowledge to their students. Advance preparation was almost nonexistent and class rehearsals rare. Although methods of instruction courses were established, improvement was limited.

Training management, from the Central Training Command, Joint General Staff, to the training center level also left much room for betterment. The Central Training Command was responsible for training at the national level but was an extremely passive headquarters with little apparent experience in supervising and administering the training command. Army training programs, subject schedules, programs of instruction, and other training literature remained outdated and in dire need of revision.

Staffing for the Central Training Command, whose mission was comparable to Headquarters, U.S. Continental Army Command, was inadequate. For example, in 1970 two officers in the Central Training Command had total responsibility for developing, reviewing, and upgrading the forty programs which were conducted at the training centers. In addition, these same officers were tasked to review all 650 programs of instruction submitted by the service schools. The job proved too great an undertaking with little being accomplished.

At the training center level, training management was no better. When revised Army training programs, subject schedules, and other training literature were received, often no real effort was made in updating and revising lesson plans so that they would correspond to the changes made. For example, four-hour blocks of instruction would be taught from two-hour lesson plans.

Hardships in such areas as class scheduling, maintenance of training records, and make-up training also existed. It was not unusual for two or three companies to show up at the same range at the same time for firing. Individual training records were almost nonexistent and reflected the cadre's resignation to the fact that many trainees would receive incomplete training. To make matters worse, there was no make-up training program.

Night training techniques also received much adverse criticism. While the Vietnamese Army programs of instruction emphasized night training, the training centers generally did not implement the instruction effectively. This situation was partly due to the practice of limiting training to a "regular" eight-hour workday and partly to the requirement for centers to furnish their own night security personnel from the training detachments.

Although the programs of instruction emphasized specialized training, such as night, small unit, and marksmanship training, these activities were often too complex for the basic Vietnamese Army soldier. Many blocks of instruction could have been eliminated or at least reduced in length. For example, much of the technical material on the functioning of the M16 rifle was wasted because the rifle was far more sophisticated than anything the trainee had ever encountered before. What good was it to teach him that the round detonation created 50,000 pounds of pressure per square inch chamber pressure? Such information was not really relevant to his need to learn to fire and maintain his weapon, was a waste of time, and took hours of instruction away from more valuable subjects.

The above deficiencies were not the only shortcomings found within the training centers nor were they indicative of every center.

But they were typical, and almost all trouble stemmed from the lack of aggressive leadership and of a highly capable cadre within the training center base.

Unit Training

Unit training was continually emphasized but rarely undertaken by the Vietnamese combat units. In-place unit training was virtually nonexistent. Vietnamese Army commanders were normally required to conduct this type of instruction between combat operations. For the most part, the Vietnamese commanders disregarded this requirement and used the time for rest and recuperation. The relationship between training and operational efficiency was generally unappreciated, and continued emphasis by advisers at all levels failed to modify the indifferent attitude toward in-place training.

Refresher training was also a requirement for many years. Under this program, Vietnamese Army units were rotated through training centers, usually once every two to three years. Training sessions lasted from four to five weeks, and unit officers and noncommissioned officers were to accompany their units while training center instructors provided the actual instruction. The arrangement was a complete failure with the major problem being the reluctance of corps and division commanders to release combat units from operational missions for refresher training. Another handicap was the attitude of the unit officers and noncommissioned officers who regarded the training period as a chance for rest and recuperation. The result was a complete lack of interest in unit retraining. Thus, while the need for unit training was valid, and the programs for retraining Vietnamese Army units in training centers by training center instructors was sound, there was need for the whole practice to be re-examined. In any case, the success of any future modifications will be greatly dependent on a grater appreciation of the value of training in a combat environment.

Military Schools

The Vietnamese armed forces school system, like the training centers, was rapidly expanded and finally totaled twenty-five different schools. U.S. advisers supervised this expansion and were assigned to each school to advise and assist in developing successful training programs. Not surprising, the resulting school system was patterned after that of the United States and gave officer and enlisted instruction at all levels of responsibility in general, technical, and administrative fields.

The establishment of this system was a continuous process tied closely to the course of the war. As new requirements were recognized, new schools were established through advisory insistence. For example, the National Defense College was established in Saigon in August 1967 in recognition of the need to provide training to top military officers and government civilians for functions involving national security; the Vietnamese National Military Academy was permanently converted from a two-year to a four-year institution in 1967 in order to improve what was the major source of regular Army officers.

Through U.S. efforts, South Vietnam has developed a school system which is probably unequaled anywhere in Asia. But, although this system is functioning and functioning well, there are still serious problem areas. Most critical are the lack of highly qualified supervisors and both highly qualified and combat-experienced instructors. Other deficiencies lie in such areas as training management, methods of instruction, and programs of instruction and are similar to those afflicting the training camps.

Summary and Conclusions

Early efforts of the United States revolved around a small number of advisers, mobile training teams, and the offshore training program. These activities were enough for the internal situation during the 1950s. At first the Americans concentrated on creating a military force which was conventional in tactics and equipment, patterned after the standard U.S. organization, and capable of withstanding an invasion from the north. This Army proved incapable of coping with an internal insurgency. Before 1960 its organization was too centralized and its equipment too heavy to counter the rapid growth of the guerrilla war.

In 1959–60 the United States realized that the development of a counterinsurgency capability was urgent. Its massive efforts to develop this capability through the use of Special Forces units, mobile training teams, increased advisory assistance, revised training programs, organizational changes and increased combat support forces, and matériel aid were extremely successful and resulted in great official optimism by 1963. But the Buddhist uprisings and the successful overthrow of the Diem regime in late 1963 led to a complete deterioration of the armed forces. Only the decision to introduce U.S. combat forces in early 1965 saved the Republic of Vietnam from total military defeat.

The years following 1965 were characterized by continuous efforts to revitalize the South Vietnam Army with men, money, and matériel. Time for these efforts was bought by the commitment of large U.S. combat forces, and for a while many U.S. leaders felt that American troops could defeat the insurgency alone. Militating against this view were two serious problems affecting the buildup and training of the Vietnamese Army. First, by 1967 the Vietnamese Army was devoted almost entirely to pacification security missions and, in the minds of many, had been relegated to a secondary role in the conduct of the war. Vietnamese Army units often reflected this attitude in their over-all lack of enthusiasm and in their willingness to leave most of the fighting to the Americans. This apathy ended during *Tet* offensive of 1968 when the Army's combat performance allowed the units to regain a sense of pride and purpose. In retrospect, the Vietnamese Army should have been given a greater combat burden between 1965 and 1968, together with more U.S. backup support.

A second problem was also a by-product of the large U.S. ground presence. By 1966 U.S. forces had been given first priority for men, money, and matériel, and the basic mission of strengthening the Vietnamese armed forces became a second priority. This change immediately lowered the quality of advisory personnel and the availability of the more modern equipment for the Vietnamese Army. By 1966 the high standards required of advisory personnel were abandoned and instead emphasis was placed on assigning the best men to U.S. combat forces in South Vietnam. Officers and noncommissioned officers began to look upon advisory duty as undesirable and avoided such duty if possible; promotions came through assignments to U.S. units, not through advisory service. Sensing this drop in adviser quality, General Westmoreland continually emphasized the importance of the advisory mission and referred to it as the "heart and soul" of the U.S. effort in Vietnam. Finally, a series of projects were undertaken to make these positions more attractive, and this series proved partially successful in re-establishing the desirability of advisory duty.

The large scale of the American involvement after 1965 also precluded extensive equipment modernization for the Vietnamese armed forces until 1968, and the practice of lending equipment to the Vietnamese Army from USARV stocks satisfied only certain priority needs. However, once the decision was made to limit U.S. involvement and Vietnamize the war, the situation changed. Beginning in 1969 vast quantities of matériel became available to the Vietnamese armed forces, most of which were supplied by redeploying U.S. units. From 1969 to 1972 American units and com-

South Vietnamese Armor in Cambodia

mands, together with the U.S. advisory network, were heavily committed to the buildup and modernization of the Vietnamese armed forces. At the same time, the armed forces training base also expanded to meet the demands of Vietnamization so that its dependence on U.S. training support was minimal by the end of 1972. While it is difficult to say if these measures should have been taken earlier, it is evident that they were implemented successfully once the South Vietnamese Army was given greater attention.

In summary, the U.S. approach in training has been successful despite the many deficiencies indicated. As concluded earlier, the whole problem revolves around the availability of qualified leadership. Although many leadership courses were established and continual emphasis placed on the development of leadership, a serious obstacle was United States own overriding emphasis on establishing "rapport" with its counterparts even at the expense of not accomplishing its mission. Too often advisers did not take firm stands with their counterparts on key issues nor recommend the relief of unsatisfactory commanders for fear that such recommendations would reflect badly on their own abilities. If more

South Vietnamese Field Operation

advisers had insisted on the relief of ineffective commanders, command positions would have opened up, affording incentive and opportunity for the more junior officers to exercise their leadership ability. The rapport approach is dangerous because it lends itself to the acceptance of substandard performance by the adviser. In any future situation where advisers are deployed under hostile conditions, the emphasis should be on getting the job done, not on merely getting along with the individual being advised.

Appendix A

MAJOR RVNAF SCHOOLS AND TRAINING CENTERS EXISTING AT THE END OF 1958

National Military Academy
Command and General Staff College
Quang Trung Replacement Training Center
English Language School
Service schools
    Armor
    Artillery
    Infantry
    Engineer
    Quartermaster
    Signal
    Transportation
    Drivers and Mechanics
    Intelligence and Psychological Warfare
    Commando
    Medical Training Center
    Signal Training Center
    Airborne

Source: History, Development of the Training Directorate, HQ, MACV (May 1970).

Appendix B

RVNAF ACADEMIES, COLLEGES, AND SCHOOLS [1]

General

Most of the formal training administered by the Central Training Command was conducted through the many and varied military academies, colleges, and schools throughout the Republic of Vietnam. Some of these institutions were relatively new while others had existed before the armed forces of South Vietnam was established, and no less than four of them—the Command and Staff College, the Noncommissioned Officers Academy, and the Engineer and Medical schools—were originally located in North Vietnam. Almost all of the major schools have at one time or another been located at and been a part of the Thu Duc Military School Center. This now-defunct center and forerunner of no less than ten schools was the hub of RVNAF training during the period immediately following the Geneva Accords of 1954. In time, the different schools expanded and most moved to other sites because Thu Duc was too small to contain the budding training base of the new South Vietnamese armed forces. These institutions continued to enlarge their facilities and develop, revise, and update their training curriculums in accordance with the emergence of the new military force. Also, new schools were instituted to broaden the training base and develop a well-rounded and well-balanced force—a military force in which all personnel, regardless of speciality, could receive formal training. A listing of the academies, colleges, and schools together with a brief history of each follows (for locations in 1969, *see Appendix C*; for enrollment in 1970, *see Appendix D*).

Vietnamese National Military Academy

The Vietnamese National Military Academy (VNMA) was founded in December 1948 in Hue. Under French operation, the academy was simply a nine-month officer training school designed to produce infantry platoon leaders. In 1950 it moved to Dalat because of better local weather and remained under French opera-

---

[1] The material in this appendix was taken from HQ, MACV, *Command History, 1969*, II, VI-81-VI-92, and *Command History, 1970*, II, VII-51-VII-55.

tion until after the signing of the Geneva Accords in 1954, when the Vietnamese assumed control. In 1955 the American advisory effort began, and the curriculum was extended to one year and in 1956 to two years. In 1959 President Diem first declared the academy to be a full four-year, degree-granting, university-level institution. Expansion planning and construction began, but the program floundered because of the conflicting short-term demand for junior officers and lack of a qualified academic faculty. As a result, the academy graduated three 3-year classes but no 4-year classes and, in 1963, reverted to the production of enlightened platoon leaders with two years of training. The concept was similar to U.S. officer candidate schools throughout 1965. In December 1966, Premier Ky issued a decree which reinstituted a four-year educational requirement, with graduates entitled to receive a Bachelor of Science degree, and changed the academy mission to the following:

> The Vietnamese National Military Academy is responsible for training regular army officers for the Armed Forces of the Republic of Vietnam who possess a university level of instruction and a firm military background.

A VNMA applicant had to be a citizen between the ages of eighteen and twenty-two, unmarried, and a high school graduate to be considered for acceptance. Appointment to the academy was based upon the results of a two-day competitive academic examination and a complete physical examination. The more highly qualified students obtained from this competition provided a basis for developing the potential of an "elite" professional corps. Approximately one out of ten applicants were accepted. In 1968, for example, out of more than 2,500 applicants only 270 were accepted in the four-year program. The attrition rate has been minimal since the academy's conversion to a four-year college, averaging from 4 to 5 percent (the approximate average rate for West Point as well as the Philippine and Korean Military academies is 30 percent). At the beginning of 1969, the academy had an enrollment of 900 cadets with plans to expand the enrollment to 1,000 by the end of the year.

By 1970 the physical plant consisted of ten buildings including four cadet dormitories, three academic buildings, an academy headquarters, a cadet mess hall, and a cadet club. Under construction were faculty quarters, a fourth academic building, a library, and a cadet regimental headquarters.

The four-year curriculum was diverse. Besides military subjects and courses in mathematics, physics, history, English, law, philosophy, chemistry, engineering, and surveying (50 percent of the academic program was devoted to engineering sciences), the curriculum furnished courses to help solve some of South Vietnam's unique problems. For example, a course in hamlet planning covered everything from where to put the village chief's house to how to drill wells for water; another course conducted in sanitary engineering was designed to improve the sanitation in hamlets and villages.

Subjects were taught by the academy's all-RVNAF military faculty of approximately 100 instructors. Classes were held as seminars with small groups of cadets. All cadets had their own textbooks which was something rare in civilian Vietnamese universities. Although the VNMA curriculum was patterned after the U.S. service academies, the cadets were exposed to more classroom hours than the cadets at West Point; however, both participated in the same amount of athletic activity.

In 1969 there were twelve U.S. military personnel in the VNMA advisory detachment. Advisory efforts were geared toward improving the quality of entering cadets, obtaining a better qualified staff and faculty, developing a balanced curriculum, and supporting the VNMA's physical expansion. The U.S. Senior Advisor noted that, although reports and comments about the VNMA graduates have been excellent, "the future of the Academy rests with how well it can keep pace with the changing situation and times. Updating texts, expanding facilities to meet needs, bettering the faculty; these are what are important."

In December 1969, the "West Point" of South Vietnam turned out the first class of ninety-two cadets to graduate from its four-year program. The event set the stage for a crucial test of one of the most ambitious plans of Vietnamization to date. During the colorful pass-in-review graduation ceremony, the long-range importance of the academy graduates was emphasized by the presence of President Thieu and a host of top political and military leaders of the country. In his remarks President Thieu told them "they must be more than military leaders" and urged the graduates to be in the forefront of a nation-building generation.

On graduation these cadets were assigned to the three services as follows: Army 77 cadets, Air Force 10, Navy/Marine Corps 5. During the period 15–20 December 1970, 196 candidates for class number 26 reported to the academy for in-processing examinations. Eight candidates were declared unfit for military service for medical reasons; 250 primary candidates and 119 alternates had been selected for the class. On 24 December, 188 fully qualified candidates were admitted as new cadets and formal training commenced.

During 1970 a cadet in his second year at the Vietnamese National Military Academy became the first Vietnamese to be accepted for entrance to the U.S. Military Academy, West Point.

National Noncommissioned Officers Academy

The National Noncommissioned Officers Academy had been founded by the French Army in 1951 in Quang Yen Province, North Vietnam, and had been called the Commando School. After the Geneva Accords of 1954, the school reverted to RVNAF control and moved to Khanh Hoa Province in II Corps Tactical Zone where its mission was changed from training commandos to that of conducting basic infantry courses. Because of the lack of space, the school moved again, this time to Nha Trang, and was renamed the Commando and Physical Training Center with the expanded mission of conducting commando, reconnaissance, antiguerrilla, physical training, boxing, judo, and basic infantry courses. In late 1958 the school was again redesignated as the National Noncommissioned Officers Academy and received the new mission of training selected noncommissioned officers in the principles of leadership and command. In 1967 the academy incorporated airmobile training courses into its curriculum, and in 1968, in order to relieve the training pressure on the Infantry School, conducted and graduated four officer candidate classes. This course was discontinued after the fourth class graduated in early 1969. Also in 1969, nine reserve noncommissioned officers courses were conducted at the academy and a tenth class began on 1 December.

During 1970, 16,522 students attended the academy, and significant progress was made in improving facilities and upgrading training. A self-help program provided one 800-man mess hall and 175 eight-man mess tables; at the same time construction continued on fifteen student barracks. With MACV approval, the academy's allocation of M16 rifles was increased from 1,000 to 3,000, the student daily food allowance was enlarged, and the receipt of a favorable contract for civilian supplied foods made available adequate rations. By May the M16 rifles were issued, which brought the total on hand to 3,000, and the fifteen new barracks were completed which increased the capacity from 3,320 men to 4,520. Greater emphasis by advisers resulted in major improvements in the quality of leadership training and day and night practical exercises. Detailed training inspections were conducted by the ARVN staff and U.S. advisers. Inspection reports were forwarded through ARVN channels and follow-up corrective actions taken. U.S. training teams from the 4th Infantry Division and 173d Airborne Brigade visited the academy to assist in improving the quality of mine and booby-trap training.

National Defense College

The National Defense College (NDC), one of the newest RVNAF schools, was established by national decree on 22 August 1967. Its dual mission was to educate outstanding and high-ranking military and career government civilians to become better qualified to perform important functions relevant to the national security and to study, plan, and develop national defense policy.

The first class, consisting of fifteen officers (0–5 and 0–6) and six high-ranking civilians, assembled on 6 May 1968; all twenty-one students completed the course and were graduated in April 1969. A second class of sixteen military and eight civilians commenced on 3 May 1969.

The curriculum of the National Defense College consisted of an orientation, ten courses, and seven seminars which fell into three major categories—international affairs, national resources, and national defense strategy—and an individual research program. In addition, the college offered an elective English program and conducted a unique senior seminar. In this weekly senior seminar, key general officers and distinguished career government officials were invited to hear important guest speakers who lectured on significant topics. Following the lecture, the guest speaker met with the regular class in a seminar on subjects related to the lecture. This procedure promoted understanding at the highest governmental level, not only of the vital topics under discussion, but also of the role of the college and how it contributed to the attainment of national goals.

Command and Staff College

The Command and Staff College (C&SC) was organized at Hanoi in 1952 when the French Expeditionary Corps established a "Tactical Instruction Center" with the mission of training mobile group, battalion, and company commanders. In late 1953 the school was transformed into the Military Research Center with a mission of providing wartime officers with accelerated training. After the Geneva Accords, the colleges moved from Hanoi to Saigon, was redesignated the Command and General Staff College, and was assigned the mission of training high-ranking officers for the Vietnamese armed forces. In 1961 the college again moved, this time to Dalat, where it occupied the buildings which had previously housed the Vietnamese National Military Academy. During 1962 and 1963, the courses of instruction had been shortened and oriented to stress counterinsurgency techniques. After the relocation to Dalat, the college expanded and battalion staff and battalion command extension (correspondence) courses were added (the battalion command course was transferred to the Infantry School in 1964). In addition, the battalion commander's combined arms course, a sixteen-week mobilization course, was inaugurated at the college in December 1965. A CTC study in early 1967 resulted in a change in the names of the residence courses, a broadened scope of instruction, and the present name for the college.

In 1969, as the senior tactical school in the country, as a joint service institution, and as the only institution (other than the National Defense College) that offered the education and prestige so vital to the developing nation, the Command and Staff College possessed a fivefold training mission:

1. to train selected field grade officers for duty as commanders at regimental and senior sector level or higher and staff officers at division level or higher;

2. to train selected captains and majors for duty as battalion commanders, district chiefs, or staff officers at battalion and regimental level;

3. to provide a limited number of Air Force, Navy, and Marine Corps officers of combat arms and technical services with sound knowledge of the armed forces in order to foster a high degree of co-ordination in joint operations;

4. to conduct an extension course for nonresident, active duty officers in grades from first lieutenant to major; and

5. to organize special courses as directed by the Joint General Staff (by the JGS directive, an officer must be a graduate of the intermediate course to be eligible for promotion to lieutenant colonel and of the advanced course for eligibility for promotion to colonel).

The curriculum of the college consisted of two separate courses of instruction—a twenty-week advanced course for majors through colonels and a twelve-week intermediate course for captains and majors. The intermediate training was also offered through a correspondence course for first lieutenants through majors. The curriculum was designed to support a joint service college, and the programs of instruction for each course were continually revised and modified to support the requirements of the armed forces and province and district leaders. A certain degree of repetition occurred between the two courses that was both necessary and desirable in providing background fundamentals, information on current development, and continuity. Both courses emphasized combined arms training appropriate to the level of the course, and continual reorganization of the programs of instruction permitted good coverage of unconventional warfare, counterinsurgency, sector and territorial security, pacification, political warfare, revolutionary development, and general subjects dealing with national and international problems. The graduation exercise of the Sixth Advanced Command and Staff Course took place on 19 December 1969, at the college auditorium and was presided over by the Chief, Central Training Command; ninety-seven students successfully completed the course and seven failed.

Political Warfare College

The history of the Political Warfare (POLWAR) College began with the establishment of a Psychological Warfare (PSYWAR) training center at Fort Cay Mai, Saigon, in 1956. Its annual output was 212 individuals in 1961, 884 in 1962, and 940 in 1963. In 1964 the training center moved to Camp Le Van Duyet in III Corps Tactical Zone, but the facilities at the new location were so inadequate that student capacity decreased from 350 to 80. This student output later grew to 150 through self-help projects, but the 1965 output was still below previous years, with only 427 students graduating.

With the advent of the political warfare structure in the armed forces, the training center was redesignated as the Political Warfare School in 1965 and in 1966 moved to its present location in Dalat. About the same time, it was upgraded to a college with the primary mission of providing a two-year college level course to train professional POLWAR officers. Political warfare cadets were recruited and sent to the Infantry School to receive basic training with OCS candidates; upon completion of basic training, they moved to Dalat to begin their POLWAR training. The members of the first class, graduated in May 1969, were assigned to POLWAR battalions and to ARVN regiments and RF companies as POLWAR advisers.

Other missions of the college included giving Branch training for RVNAF officers and organizing and directing POLWAR specialist training as required. The 1968 quotas for the course at the POLWAR College included 379 cadets for the two-year program and 475 students in shorter, three-month courses for POLWAR Branch training.

Infantry School

Originally called the Thu Duc Reserve Officers School, the Infantry School had been established at Thu Duc in October 1951 along with its sister school in Nam Dinh, North Vietnam. Both schools were originally administered by the French Army, and all instruction took place in French. In 1952, after the closing of the Nam Dinh Reserve Officers School, the Thu Duc school became the only reserve officer producing school in Vietnam. In 1954, after the Geneva Accords, the management of the school changed from the French to the Vietnamese armed forces.

In 1955 the Infantry School was given the job of training cadres and specialists of other branches of the Vietnamese Army in addition to the infantry. Its name was then changed to the Thu Duc Military School Center and comprised the Infantry, Armor, Artillery, Engineer, Signal, Ordnance, Transportation, and Administrative schools. In October 1961 all of these schools, with the exception of Infantry and Armor, moved from the Thu Duc area to provide space for the greatly expanded ARVN Reserve Officers Procurement Program.

After several name changes associated with its changing mission, the Thu Duc Reserve Officers School was officially renamed the Infantry School during July 1964. After that the school expanded until, at the end of 1967, it had a capacity of 3,800 students. Its training program included the officer candidate, company commander, RF officer refresher, and methods of instruction courses. Following the enemy *Tet* offensive in 1968, all courses were temporarily canceled, except for the two officer candidate cycles.

In June 1968 a dramatic change occurred in the school's curriculum and training program. To meet increased officer requirements as a result of the general mobilization, the capacity was increased to approximately 6,000 students. At the same time, the length of the officer candidate program was decreased from thirty-seven to twenty-four weeks; the first nine weeks consisted of basic and advanced individual training at the Quang Trung Training Center and the rest of the training was conducted at the school.

Since becoming an officer-producing school in 1952, the Infantry School has graduated over 40,900 students as of November 1969 and continued to be the largest source of officers in the Vietnamese armed forces. The importance of its mission and the success of its graduates made the school notable as one of the most important military installations in South Vietnam.

By 1970 the Infantry School was beginning to realize the benefits of the special construction program to upgrade facilities. Nine classrooms were constructed and furniture was received to accommodate 200 students in each of the nine classrooms. Increased emphasis was placed on instructor training and the methods of instruction course was revised to emphasize practical application as opposed to the lecture system. The first of the new methods of instruction courses at the Infantry School graduated eighty-seven students.

Much headway was also made in new construction, rehabilitation of barracks and messes, development of specialized training areas, and competition among units. A signal training area was constructed for more practical application in communications training. Terrain models, mock-ups, and bleachers were constructed to improve map reading and weapons training. Work was started on a mock-up Viet Cong hamlet, a physical fitness combat proficiency test area, and a platoon defensive area. A unit competition program was implemented encompassing academic scores, barracks and unit area inspections, physical training, marching, and intramural sports.

Artillery School

The RVNAF Artillery School was an outgrowth of the French Army's Artillery Training Center of Indochina located in Phu Hoa. After the signing of the Geneva Accords, the training center was turned over to the Vietnamese armed forces and was redesignated the RVNAF Artillery School. In October 1955 the school moved to the Thu Duc Military School Center and shared its facilities with the Engineer School; when the Engineer School moved out two years later, the Artillery School took over the entire area. With this additional space, the school was reorganized and the training activities expanded. In July 1961 the school moved again, this time to its present location in Duc My, where it was again reorganized with its own administrative and logistic support.

Throughout its existence, the school has trained artillery officers and noncommissioned officers in the operation and maintenance of all artillery equipment and has also conducted basic and advanced unit training for ARVN artillery battalions as they were activated under the RVNAF Improvement and Modernization programs. A four-week counterbattery course was established at the school, along with two AN/MPQ/4A radar sets and equipment in 1969. Then, the rated capacity of the school was 600 students. During December the student load reached 1,086, severely straining facilities and instructors. The overload was a result of the requirement to train additional personnel to fill newly activated units and units scheduled for activation. Under these overcrowded conditions, the amount of practical work done and personal supervision received was greatly reduced, adversely affecting the quality of graduates.

In 1970 several new gun emplacements with concrete personnel shelters and ammunition bunkers were built in the battalion demonstration area as a self-help project. New programs of instruction were prepared for a survey officer course and a survey instructor course. A copy of the U.S. Artillery Advanced Course was obtained from Fort Sill, edited to delete unusable portions, and given to the director of instruction for upgrading the battalion commander's course. In addition, noticeable improvements in training and supervision of students took place after the commandant directed that classes be inspected daily and written reports submitted.

One of the most significant improvements in training occurred between April and June 1970. Formerly, no attempt was made to co-ordinate the training of forward observers, fire direction center personnel, and gun crews during live fire exercises. During June, schedules and programs of instruction were completed to allow these classes to be conducted simultaneously. The concept saved ammunition and training time and released support troop gun crews to perform maintenance.

Armor School

The Armor School was first established by the French Army at the Vietnamese Military Academy in Dalat in 1950 and was staffed by French officers and Vietnamese enlisted men. In late 1952 the school was dissolved and its functions taken over by the Thu Duc Reserve Officers School. Then, in February 1955, when the Thu Duc Reserve Officers School became the Thu Duc Military School Center, the armor portion was again established as a separate school. Finally, when the other schools of the training center moved to their new locations in October 1961, the Armor School became an independent entity under the Armor Command and has remained so ever since.

The mission of the school was to train armor personnel in the use and tactics of all armor-type vehicles found in the RVNAF inventory. It also conducted basic and advanced unit training for all newly activated ARVN armor units to ensure that they were combat ready before going into the field as operational forces.

On 13 December 1969, construction of a tank gunnery range

was completed at Trang Bom. The range, approximately forty kilometers from the school, permitted trainees to fire main batteries without having to travel excessive distances to tank ranges under U.S. or Australian operational control.

Signal School

The Signal School had been originally the Communications Training Center of the French Army in Indochina and was located in Gia Dinh. In 1954 it became the ARVN Signal Communications Training Center and consisted of two separate centers —the Signal School in Thu Duc, whose primary goal was training signal officers for the Vietnamese Army and enlisted men of all services in signal equipment repair, and the Signal Training Center in Vung Tau, whose primary mission was training RVNAF enlisted men in the use of all types of communications equipment.

In October 1961 the Thu Duc portion of the school was transferred to and consolidated with the Vung Tau portion in their present location. The consolidated portion was designated the RVNAF Signal School and given the combined mission that had previously been assigned both centers. In August the school's organization expanded to include personnel and equipment for a cryptographic facility for training all RVNAF students in the use of the new cipher equipment.

On 28 February 1970 a large portion of land formerly occupied by U.S. elements of the Vung Tau Sub-area Command was turned over to the Signal School. Located about 1,000 meters from the main compound, the area had room for 1,200 people and was complete with buildings. The complex was used to billet the Language School students preparing for entrance into the Integrated Communications System (ICS) training program. In December members of the first fixed station microwave repair course graduated. The military occupational specialty (MOS) involved was one of the most complex in the ICS program and was awarded only after thirteen months of intensive instruction conducted by the U.S. 369th Signal Battalion.

Engineer School

The Engineer School began as a training center near Haiphong, North Vietnam. Here the French maintained an engineer center with the responsibility of instructing and training Vietnamese engineer soldiers. In 1951, in order to train Vietnamese engineer officers, the center was moved to and became part of the

Thu Duc Reserve Officers School. Three years later the school was turned over to the Vietnamese, and the Engineer Training Center moved to Bien Hoa. In September 1955 it moved back to Thu Duc and was designated as the Engineer School; here the entire family of courses in military engineering, from basic training to generalized education, was developed and presented.

Because of the need for expanded facilities and more adequate training areas, the school moved to Vung Tau in October 1957. In its new site, more sophisticated courses were developed, including specialized operator courses for all types of engineer equipment. The student capacity at Vung Tau was 400 officers and men.

In August 1961 the school closed and moved to its present location at Phu Cuong in Binh Duong Province. Classes resumed in January 1962, and since then the school has trained officers, officer candidates, noncommissioned officers, and enlisted personnel of the RVNAF Corps of Engineers in the techniques, procedures, and methods of military engineering. The training mission was based on the concept of making and development of combat engineers through courses on engineer equipment operation, first and second echelon maintenance, and engineer management.

Because of the post-1965 buildup, the 1,000-student capacity of Phu Cuong became inadequate and the Engineer School developed a five-year plan to increase its capacity to 3,000. The Central Training Command's Upgrading Plan considered relocating the Engineer School, but Central Training Command decided to keep the school at the present location and expand the facilities over a five-year period.

Military Police School

The Military Police School was organized as a training center in Da Nang in 1957, the same year that the ARVN Military Police Corps was established. Its goal was conducting basic military police training courses at a rate of five 12-week courses every two years. Each class consisted of approximately 250 individuals, and graduates were initially assigned only to I Corps Tactical Zone; later, assignments were made to units throughout the country. In April 1962 the center moved to its present site at Vung Tau and was renamed the RVNAF Military Police School.

In January 1965 the school's organization was expanded to include personnel and equipment for a criminal investigation laboratory which was responsible for scientific analysis of evidence submitted by field units and for the training of criminal investigators. The laboratory did not become operational until much later, however.

The school received an approved expansion plan for the 1967–69 period which permitted training of 500 students at a time. This Plan included the training of Military Police Corps junior officers, noncommissioned officers, and criminal investigators. The school also conducted the basic combat training course for all recruits assigned to the Military Police Corps.

On 28 February 1970, an 18,000-square-meter tract was transferred to the Military Police School by U.S. elements of the Vung Tau Sub-area Command. The land adjacent to the school was used for riot control training, an enlarged motor pool, recreation facilities, and a hardstand helicopter pad.

Administrative Schools

In October 1955 the Vietnamese armed forces established the Military Administration School at the Thu Duc Military School Center with the mission of providing specialized training in quartermaster, finance and administration, and personnel administration subjects. In 1958 as the program expanded and student capacities were raised, it became necessary to reorganize the school into two separate branches—the Finance and Administration Branch and the Quartermaster Branch. The arrangement proved satisfactory until 1962 when it was decided, as a result of a lack of space and the rapid expansion of the different branches, to divide the institution into three separate schools. The Adjutant General's School was established in March 1962 and the Quartermaster School and Administration and Finance School in July 1962; all three were located in Saigon where they trained specialists in their respective fields.

Transportation School

The Transportation School dates from 1954 when a highway transport officers basic course was organized and conducted at the Thu Duc Reserve Officers Training Center. Officers were transferred into this course upon completion of their infantry training. In February 1955 the Highway Transport School was officially activated as part of the Thu Duc Center and two months later was made a separate school under the supervision of the newly established Transportation Command. The school's mission of training drivers, organizational mechanics, and noncommissioned officers made an expansion of facilities necessary, and in January

1957 the school was temporarily split. The regional driver and second echelon mechanic courses moved to the Quang Trung Training Center and the rest of the school remained at Thu Duc. Finally, in September 1958, the school was consolidated back into one location—the Quang Trung Training Center area—fourteen kilometers northwest of Saigon. The school's mission remained essentially the same as when it was established in 1955, but it now had an increased training capacity of 700 students. During 1969 the school advisory detachment was increased from one to three persons.

Ordnance School

The Ordnance School was first established in 1952 as the Materiel Training Center at Thu Duc. Its mission, like other branch-type schools, was to train ordnance personnel in their specialty. In 1957 it was redesignated as the Ordnance School and retained its primary training mission. In 1961 the school was separated from the Thu Duc Center and moved to Saigon where it conducted sixty-eight different courses in ordnance specialities to satisfy the growing RVNAF demands.

Medical School

A small medical school had been established in 1951 at Hanoi to give the Vietnamese medical battalion under French command its first formal medical training capability. The objective of this school was to train regular medical officers, pharmacists, and dentists. The school moved to Saigon in 1954 and, in 1956, was combined with the Medical Training Center whose mission consisted of training enlisted medics and NCO medical specialists. The combined institution was officially redesignated the Military Medical School in 1961. Shortly thereafter, planning was instituted to construct a modern facility which would enable the school to meet the growing medical requirements of the South Vietnamese armed forces. This facility, constructed in the Phu Tho area of Saigon, was completed and operational in April 1964 and conducted thirty-five different courses in varying medical specialties.

The enlarged Medical School conducted all battalion surgeon assistant, medical supply, and enlisted formal technical training, with the exception of basic medical training of aidmen for Regional and Popular Forces units. It did not provide training for physicians or dentists. By 1970, 3,517 students had received training.

The teaching methods used at the school were didactic and

graduates lacked practical experience. Improvement in teaching techniques, including additional use of training aids and group discussion, was urged and plans were submitted to expand the capacity of the school from 1,000 students to 3,000, to include additional billeting and classroom facilities. It was also proposed to establish an RVNAF teaching hospital on the grounds where selected graduates would receive advanced training in a controlled teaching environment under surgical, laboratory, X-ray, operating room, and nursing specialists. However, as of 1972 many serious deficiencies still remained.

Military Intelligence School

The RVNAF Military Intelligence School was established in 1955 at historic Fort Cay Mai in the Saigon–Gia Dinh area with the mission of training the intelligence platoons and squads of the South Vietnamese Army. In 1962 its mission was enlarged to include training intelligence units of the Regional Forces, but this task was withdrawn in October 1967. In 1968 the school instituted an aerial intelligence interpreter's course and graduated its first class in September. The following April the combined intelligence course seminars were begun, attended by ARVN intelligence personnel and their U.S. counterparts; later in July, interrogation of prisoners of war and order of battle courses were also instituted. These courses had previously been conducted offshore in Okinawa. The normal programed input to the combined intelligence course was 30 students per class (15 Vietnamese and 15 American). The program's objective was to give all subsector (district) S–2 personnel a short, specialized intelligence course and this objective was achieved with the completion of the final class in December. A total of 534 officers attended the four-day courses and received instruction designed to enhance the exchange of intelligence information on a daily basis.

In 1970 the school enrolled a total of 2,199 students and developed three new courses dealing with collection, intermediate intelligence, and intermediate security. The collection course of thirty officers assigned to province units was conducted during January. The first intermediate officer mid-career course started in March.

Logistics Management School

The RVNAF Logistics Management School was started in 1959 but was not officially dedicated until March 1960. The mission of the school was twofold:

1. to provide high-level logistics instruction for the Vietnamese armed forces.

2. to research, study, and develop logistics organization and doctrine for the Vietnamese armed forces.

The school offered three levels of instruction, each designed to cover a specific portion of the over-all logistics system in the Vietnamese armed forces. The logistics management course concentrated on preparing selected officers for staff duties. The logistics staff officers course prepared officers to work at the intermediate level and the supply officers course prepared officers to work at unit level. During 1969 two new programs of instruction were added: The PRAISE (Program Review and Analysis Improvement Systems Evaluation) course and the U.S. Advisor Orientation course. Also, the school's capacity grew from 125 to 175 students.

Army Social Training School

The Army Social Training School in Saigon was established unofficially in October 1952 and provided basic and advanced technical training in social welfare to Women of the Armed Forces Corps (WAFC) officers and noncommissioned officers whose actual or anticipated assignment was as a social service assistant in the RVNAF Social Service Department. In addition, the school provided technical refresher training for civilian kindergarten teachers administered by the Social Service Department and gave other appropriate technical training as directed by the Joint General Staff.

Armed Forces Language School

The Vietnamese Armed Forces Language School opened in Saigon in June 1956 with the mission of teaching English to Vietnamese who were programed to attend offshore schooling in the United States. Its capacity at that time was about 1,000 students. In July 1967 the school doubled its input by increasing facilities and operating on a two-shift basis. The school's mission was then expanded to include training of Vietnamese translators for requirements within the country. During the *Tet* offensive of 1968, 70 percent of the school's facilities were destroyed; however, new facilities were obtained and the training continued almost without interruption. As the Vietnamese armed forces grew and the requirement for offshore schooling increased, the school enlarged its facilities until, by the end 1968, it had a capacity of 5,000 students.

Offshore trainees who graduated from the school had an excellent (rated "70 percent") language capability and attended U.S. schools without the previously required three-month TDY period of English schooling in CONUS.

An additional facility for the school was established at Vung Tau by renovating the Kiet Compound building to make possible a capacity of 660 students. The facility was completed on 5 December, and the first class began three days later. Four hundred and sixty-four ARVN Signal Corps students entered the class to learn English in preparation for further training in the ICS program.

During 1970 the school established a MACV Test Control Office to centralize control, security, and administration of English language comprehension and aptitude tests. Before organizing this office, the English Comprehension Level (ECL) test was often compromised, and there was approximately a thirty-point drop in a student's ECL score between the final test administered in Vietnam and the entry test administered at the Defense Language Institute, English Language School, Lackland Air Force Base. The Test Control Office eliminated test irregularities, forcing students to achieve the ECL score required for graduation legitimately.

Annex 1 (Dong Khanh) of the language school was transferred to the Adjutant General's School on 16 January 1970, and the capacity of the annex was increased from 420 to 1,000 students. Annex 2 (Tan Son Nhut) commenced training on 19 January 1970 for VNAF airmen with a capacity of 1,080 students.

Band School

The RVNAF Band School was founded in Saigon in February 1959, owing mainly to the efforts of the incumbent bandmaster. Originally, it was known as the Army Band Center and shortly after establishment developed a training program of basic and intermediate courses. In 1961 it was renamed the RVNAF Music School and moved to Thu Duc where it continued to train musicians for the twenty RVNAF bands. In December, at the request of the Senior Advisor, the English translation of the Vietnamese school was changed to "RVNAF Band School."

Junior Military Academy

The first junior military school was established in Vung Tau in 1915 under the French and was later relocated to Gia Dinh and My Tho. Similar schools had also been established in Mong Cay,

Hue, Hanoi, Ban Me Thuot, Song Mao, and Thu Dau Mot, all supported by the French. The RVNAF Junior Military Academy was activated in 1956 at Vung Tau bringing together at a single location the several junior military schools once located in Central and South Vietnam. Since 1956 the Junior Military Academy has been supported and administered by the government of Vietnam. By the end of 1969 the Central Training Command provided the instructors and facilities, and the Ministry of Education established the curriculum and the program instruction.

The mission of the school was to provide secondary education and military training to the sons of the Vietnamese military, Regional and Popular Forces, and police and village administration personnel who had served or had given their lives in the war.

The academic year began on 15 September and ended on 30 June. The courses taught included an elementary school course, a junior high school and a senior high school course, and military basic training. Ages of the students ranged from twelve through eighteen.

Appendix C

RVNAF Training School Enrollments for 1970

In calendar year 1970 the Republic of Vietnam armed forces trained 503,740 men in thirty-three national, Regional and Popular Forces, and division training centers and 87,197 men in fifteen technical, four academic, and four combat arms schools.

Principal School Enrollments for 1970

School	Programed Input	Actual Input	Percentage
AG	5,210	4,959	95
Admin & Fin	1,270	921	73
AFLS	11,236	9,622	86
Armor	5,225	5,605	107
Arty	1,715	2,327	136
Band	475	342	72
C&SC	1,000	843	84
Engineer	5,673	6,571	116
Infantry	10,762	11,929	111
Intelligence	1,523	2,199	144
JMA	1,400	1,371	98
Log Mgt	810	873	108
Mil Dog Training Ctr	310	308	102
MP	1,222	1,908	156
Medical	2,300	3,517	153
NDC	40	26	65
NCO Acad	20,960	16,522	79
Ordnance	2,918	2,570	88
POLWAR	505	304	60
QM	1,539	1,436	93
Signal	8,931	5,702	64
Social Welfare	580	199	34
Trans	8,894	11,029	124
VNMA	250	191	76
WAFC	1,400	1,025	73

Source: HQ, MACV, *Command History, 1970,* II, V–II–56.

Appendix D

REPUBLIC OF VIETNAM ARMED FORCES STRENGTH [a]

	Army	Air Force	Navy	Marine Corps	Total Regular	Regional Forces	Popular Forces	Total Territorial	Grand Total
1954–55	170,000	3,500	2,200	1,500	177,200	54,000 [b]	48,000 [b]	102,000	279,200
1959–60	136,000 [c]	4,600	4,300	2,000	146,000	49,000 [c]	48,000	97,000	243,000
1964	220,000	11,000	12,000	7,000	250,000	96,000	168,000	264,000	514,000
1967	303,000	16,000	16,000	8,000	343,000	151,000	149,000 [c]	300,000	643,000
1968	380,000	19,000	19,000	9,000	427,000	220,000	173,000	393,000	820,000
1969	416,000	36,000	30,000	11,000	493,000	190,000	214,000	404,000	897,000
1970	416,000	46,000	40,000	13,000	515,000	207,000	246,000	453,000	968,000
1971–72	410,000 [c]	50,000	42,000	14,000	516,000	284,000	248,000	532,000	1,048,000

[a] All figures are approximate only.
[b] Civil Guard (later Regional Forces) and Self-Defense Corps (later Popular Forces) were officially authorized only in 1956.
[c] Decline due to increased desertions and recruiting shortfalls.

Glossary

ARPA	Advanced Research Projects Agency
ARVN	Army of the Republic of (South) Vietnam
CAS	Controlled American Source
CIDG	Civilian Irregular Defense Group
CINCPAC	Commander in Chief, Pacific (U.S. Joint Theater Command)
CIP	Counterinsurgency Plan
COMUSMACV	Commander, U.S. Military Assistance Command, Vietnam
CONUS	Continental United States
CRIMP	Consolidated Phase of the Republic of Vietnam Armed Forces Improvement and Modernization Program
C&SC	Command and Staff College (Vietnamese)
CTA	Central Training Agency
CTC	Central Training Command (Vietnamese Joint General Staff)
CTZ	Corps tactical zone
DA	Department of the Army
FEC	French Expeditionary Corps
ICC	International Control Commission
ICS	Integrated Communications System
ISD	Instructional System Development
JCS	Joint Chiefs of Staff (U.S.)
JGS	Joint General Staff (Vietnamese)
JOC	Joint operations center
MAAG	Military Assistance Advisory Group
MAAGV	Military Assistance Advisory Group, Vietnam
MAC	Military Assistance Command
MACMA	Military Assistance Command, Military Assistance
MACV	Military Assistance Command, Vietnam (a joint U.S. command)
MAP	Military Assistance Program
MASF/MILCON	Military Assistance Service Funded/Military Construction (Program)
MDAP	Mutual Defense Assistance Program
MMT	Middle Management Training (Program)
MTT	Mobile training team

NCO	Noncommissioned officer
NDC	National Defense College
NVA	North Vietnamese Army
OCS	Officer candidate school
OSD	Office of the Secretary of Defense (U.S.)
PF	Popular Forces (formerly Self-Defense Corps)
POLWAR	Political warfare (a form of psychological operations)
PRAISE	Program Review and Analysis Improvement Systems Evaluation
RD	Rural development (formerly revolutionary development)
RF	Regional Forces (formerly Civil Guard)
RVN	Republic of (South) Vietnam
RVNAF	Republic of (South) Vietnam armed forces
ST	Son Truong (similar to RD cadre)
TDY	Temporary duty
TERM	Temporary Equipment Recovery Mission
TRIM	Training Relations and Instructions Mission
USAID	U.S. Agency for International Development
USARPAC	U.S. Army, Pacific
USARV	U.S. Army, Vietnam
USCONARC	U.S. Continental Army Command
USIS	U.S. Information Service
USMACV	U.S. Military Assistance Command, Vietnam
USOM	U.S. Operations Mission
UHF	Ultrahigh frequency
VHF	Very high frequency
VIS	Vietnamese Information Service
VNAF	South Vietnam Air Force
VNMA	South Vietnamese Military Academy
VNMC	South Vietnam Marine Corps
VNN	South Vietnam Navy
VNSF	South Vietnam Special Forces
WAFC	Women's Armed Forces Corps (Vietnamese)

Index

Abrams, General Creighton W.: 89, 93–94, 109–10. *See also* United States Military Assistance Command, Vietnam.
Absences without leave: 61–62
Accelerated Model Plan, U.S.: 29–30
Adjutant General's School: 61
Administration practices: 23, 31, 61, 73, 120, 122, 127
Administration schools: 144
Advanced Research Projects Agency, U.S.: 110
Advisers and advisory groups. *See also* by name.
   in civil affairs and civic action: 45–46, 53
   in combat units: 17, 24, 26, 35, 46, 53–54, 68, 119–22, 129–30
   control of: 27, 52–53
   missions assigned: 1–2, 17, 23, 26, 30, 50–54, 58, 62, 75, 78, 80, 95, 109–10, 120, 123, 126–28
   mobile teams: 119–22, 127
   numbers authorized and assigned: 8, 22, 24, 26–27, 30–31, 39, 45, 48–53, 55, 73, 82–84, 105, 109, 123, 127
   school for: 121
   territorial assignments: 24, 46, 49, 51–52, 54, 122
Agreements, international: 1–2, 21, 23
Agricultural programs: 50
Air operations. *See* Airmobile operations; Fighter aircraft support; Strategic air support; Tactical air support.
Airborne Brigade, 173d: 118
Airborne units: 9, 13, 54–55, 91, 100–101, 119
Aircraft, fixed-wing: 54
   supply to RVN: 24, 91
   U.S. losses: 48
Air-Ground Operations Mobile Training Team: 38

Air-ground support. *See* Tactical air support.
Airlifts, of troops and supplies: 21, 24, 26, 32, 36
Airmobile divisions
   1st Cavalry: 54, 119
   101st Airborne: 118
Airmobile operations: 36–38, 109
Ambush tactics: 104, 120
Amnesty programs: 62. *See also* Repatriation program.
An Phu: 74
Apache Force: 54
Armor School: 109, 110, 141–42
Armor units: 9, 35, 68, 103
Armored personnel carriers: 35
Arms and Service Directorates: 3
Army, Department of the, U.S.: 44, 105
Army Social Training School: 147
Artillery fire support: 37
Artillery School: 140–41
Artillery units and equipment: 9, 13, 35, 103, 118
Assassinations: 17
Associate-unit program: 62–63

Band School: 148
Bao Dai: 8
Barrier systems: 120
Battlefield laborers: 62
Battlefield promotions: 100
Bearcat Camp: 108–10
Binh Gia: 47
Biological operations. *See* Chemical-biological-radiological operations.
Bolton, Brigadier General Donnelly P.: 53, 105
Bomber offensive: *See* Strategic air support.
Booz-Allen Applied Research, Inc.: 110
Border patrol: 39, 41
Bridge construction and repair: 13, 111

Buddhist uprisings: 30, 127
BUDDY Operation: 115
Bulldozers: 103
Buon Ea Yang: 74

Cambodia: 1–2, 4, 20, 108–09, 119
Camp Holloway: 48
Canada: 1, 7
Cantonment program: 65
Career management: 76, 98
Casualties
  RVN: 23, 60, 67
  U.S.: 48
Cat Lai Project: 94
Cease-fire accords: 103
Central Highlands: 9, 40, 118
Central Political Warfare Agency: 91
Central Training Command: 83, 105–10, 124–25
Chau Doc Province: 74
Chemical-biological-radiological operations: 25
Chinh, Major General Phan Trong, ARVN: 110–11
Chup Rubber Plantation: 110
Civil action programs: 25, 40, 44, 53, 55
Civil affairs
  mobile training teams: 39, 43–45
  operations and units: 21, 33, 43–46, 51
Civil Affairs Group, 97th: 45
Civil Affairs School, U.S.: 43–44
Civil defense program: 57
Civil Guard: 8–10, 13, 18–20, 22, 24–26, 29–30, 39–43
Civilian Irregular Defense Groups: 29–30, 39–41, 45, 53–55, 74–75, 91, 101
Civilians
  control of and support by: 19, 29, 47, 49, 53, 86
  government employees: 93, 95
  specialists and technicians: 4, 12, 25–26
Civil-military liaison: 44
Clear-and-hold operations: 53
Collins, General J. Lawton: 2
Combat Development and Research Center, JGS: 25
Combat effectiveness and readiness: 17, 29–33, 35–36, 46–47, 53, 62–63, 67, 84, 88, 90, 121–22, 124, 126, 128
Combined Action Program: 117–18, 120
Combined Arms Doctrinal Manual: 109–10

Combined arms training: 109–10
Combined operations: 117–19
Command and control: 9–12, 18–22, 31–32, 41–42, 66, 72–73, 117–18
Command and General Staff College, U.S. Army: 83
Command and Staff College: 14, 76–77, 79, 83, 98, 136–38
Command Leadership Committee: 76
Command post exercises: 109
Commander in Chief, Pacific. See Felt, Admiral Harry D.; United States Pacific Command.
Commando Training Center: 12, 38–39
Commerce, development of: 95
Commissary system: 61, 63–65
Communications equipment and units: 10, 18, 26, 33, 36, 42, 49, 101–02, 104, 110–11. See also Signal units.
Comprehensive Plan for South Vietnam: 29
Conscription programs: 12, 42, 56–58, 68–70, 85–86. See also Manpower procurement, retention and use.
Constabulary force: 73–74
Construction programs: 34–35, 83, 108, 111
Continental Army Command, U.S.: 38–39, 125
Contractors, civilian: 63, 111
Controlled American Source: 28, 39–41
Corps, XXIV: 118
Corps tactical zones
  I: 9, 55, 69, 90, 118
  II: 9, 54, 70, 75, 118
  III: 9, 60, 70, 108, 119
  IV: 45, 55, 57, 68, 108
Cost-of-living allowances: 93
Counterinsurgency
  plans and operations: 18–22, 24–25, 27, 29–30
  training for: 12, 15–16, 30, 33–36, 127
Country Team, U.S.: 8, 20–21, 45
Crypto-Log Support Center, U.S.: 112

Da Nang: 9, 38–39, 48, 65
Dalat: 14
Darlac Province: 74
Death gratuities: 93
Decorations and awards: 92
Defectors, enemy. See Repatriation program.

INDEX

Defense, Department of, U.S.: 7, 20–21, 39. *See also* McNamara, Robert S.
Delta Force: 54
Demilitarized zone: 103
Democratic Republic of Vietnam. *See* North Vietnam.
Department of Housing: 65
Dependents, welfare of: 60–61, 63–64, 93
Deputy Chief of Air Staff for Materiel: 11
Deputy Secretary of Defense, U.S.: 87, 89
Desertions: 9, 23, 30, 33, 46–47, 59–63, 67, 72, 74, 84, 91–93
Di An: 121
Diem, Ngo Dinh: 1–2, 10–12, 17, 19, 22–23, 28, 30, 47, 127
Director of Air Technical Service: 11
Director General of Administration, Budget, and Comptroller: 11
Director of Mobilization: 57, 59
District advisers and staffs: 49–51
Dong Tien Program: 119
Draft: *See* Conscription programs; Manpower procurement, retention and use; Recruiting programs.
Draft evaders: 58, 63
Drop zones: 54
Duc My: 34
Dulles, John Foster: 2. *See also* State, Department of, U.S.

Economic assistance program: 25, 30, 50, 63–65, 95–96
Education Consultants, Ltd.: 94
Educational programs: 50
Efficiency reports: 76
Eisenhower, Dwight D.: 1–2
Electronics. *See* Communications equipment and units.
Ely, General Paul, French Army: 3
Employment programs: 96
Engineer School: 111–12, 142–43
Engineer units: 7, 13, 39, 45–46, 50–51, 103, 111–12, 120
English Language School: 15
ENHANCE Project: 102
Enrollment, schools: 150
Equipment. *See* Matériel; *see also by name.*
Ethnic groups: 20, 40
Ewell, Lieutenant General Julian J.: 119

Expantion of RVN forces: 19–20, 22–23, 25–26, 29, 33–34, 65–71, 84, 88–91, 129

FAIRFAX Operation: 117
Families. *See* Dependents, welfare of.
Felt, Admiral Harry D.: 28. *See also* United States Pacific Command.
Field Force, II: 119
Fighter aircraft support: 37–38
Financial assistance program: 22, 27, 55–56. *See also* Economic assistance program.
Flanagan, Brigadier General Edward M., Jr.: 52
Food losses, enemy: 64
Fortifications, training in: 120
France: 1–6, 8, 11, 13, 15
Franco-American Training Relations and Instructions Mission: 1–7, 9
Free World Military Assistance Forces: 73
Freund, Brigadier General John F.: 117

Gallantry Cross: 92
General Reserve: 101
General Staff: 3, 10–11
Geneva Accords: 1–2, 4, 6–7, 9
Gia Dinh Province: 117
Government employees: 93, 95
Grenade launchers: 101
Guerrilla operations, enemy: 85, 127

Hamlet militia: 41
Harkins, General Paul D.: 28, 30. *See also* United States Military Assistance Command, Vietnam.
Hawaii: 39
Hawaii conference: 24, 32, 50, 71
Heath, Donald R.: 2, 7, 8n, 16, 19. *See also* United States Embassy.
Heiser, Major General Joseph M., Jr.: 115
Helicopter units, U.S. Army: 26, 88
Helicopters. *See also* Aircraft, fixed-wing.
  CH–34 Choctaw: 21
Helicopters—Continued
  control of: 113
  H–34: 54, 113
  supply by. *See* Airlifts, of troops and supplies.
  supply to ARVN: 24, 91, 113
  tactical use: 36–38, 52, 54

"Homesteaders": 124
Honolulu conference: 24, 32, 50, 71
Hop Tac program: 32–33
Hospitalization, veterans: 95
Housing programs: 60–61, 63, 65
Hue: 85
Hunter-killer teams: 54

Illumination, battlefield: 38
Incentive pay: 93–94
India: 1, 7
Indochina. *See* North Vietnam.
Industry, development of: 95–96
Infantry Brigade, 199th Light: 117, 119
Infantry divisions. *See also* Troop units.
  mission and training: 4, 13
  number, organization and strength: 9
Infantry Divisions, U.S. Army
  1st: 62, 119
  4th: 118
  23d (Americal): 118
  25th: 39, 62, 119
Infantry School: 108–09, 110, 139–40
Inflation, effects and control: 56, 65, 68
Information programs: 50, 55, 62, 91–92
Inspector General: 78
Instructors, shortage of and training: 16, 105–06, 123–24, 126–27
Integrated Communications System, U.S. Army: 111–12
Intelligence operations and reports: 10, 18, 20–21, 24–25, 27, 33, 38, 40, 50, 54
Internal Security Council: 19
International Control Commission: 1, 4, 6–8, 12
International Cooperation Administration: 19

Job placements and referrals: 96
Johnson, Lyndon B.: 22
Joint Chiefs of Staff, U.S.: 2, 18, 20, 26–28, 53, 69, 88–90, 101
Joint General Staff: 19, 21, 26, 62, 65, 67, 69–74, 77, 80, 82–84, 91–94, 98–100, 105, 109, 125
Joint Operations Center, JGS: 29
Joint Operations Staff, ARVN: 21
Joint Unconventional Warfare Task Force: 28
Junior Military Academy: 148–49
Junk Force: 26

Kennedy, John F.: 21–25, 28
Kit Carson Scouts: 91
Korean War experience: 12
Krek: 110
Ky, Hguyen Cao: 55, 80, 84

Landing zones: 54
Language barrier, overcoming: 16, 36, 80, 113, 116
Language School: 147–48
Laos: 1, 4, 20, 40, 109
LAW (light antitank weapon): 101
Leaders, lack of and training: 4, 15–16, 23, 46, 63, 66, 69–70, 75–84, 97–100, 104, 123–24, 126, 129–30
Leave policies: 60–61, 92
Lee, Major General Richard M.: 75–76
Liaison procedures: 36, 49, 105, 118
Light antitank weapon (LAW): 101
Lines of communication, enemy: 54
Living standard, improving: 60–61
Logistical Command, 1st: 115
Logistical Management School: 110–11, 146–47
Logistical operations and units
  ARVN: 4–5, 7, 18, 20–21, 26, 33, 69, 73, 87–88, 103, 109–11, 115, 120, 122
  U.S.: 5, 23, 27–28, 32, 87, 101
Long Binh: 112

McGarr, Lieutenant General Lionel C.: 18–19. *See also* United States Military Assistance Advisory Group, Vietnam.
Machine guns and mounts: 101–02
McNamara, Robert S.: 24, 28, 32, 40, 50, 55, 66, 69, 88, 90, 101. *See also* Defense, Department of, U.S.
Maintenance and repair: 6–7, 110–11
Management, training in: 110–11, 125, 127
Maneuvers: 13
Manila conference: 73
Manpower procurement, retention and use: 56–60, 65–72, 74, 85–87, 121. *See also* Conscription programs; Recruiting programs.
Marksmanship training: 104, 125
Martial law: 30
Matériel
  enemy: 47
  losses, ARVN: 17, 55
  status, needs and supply: 4–7, 24, 27,

29, 42, 47, 55–56, 68, 70, 88, 90, 100–103, 115–16, 127–29
Medical civic action programs: 45
Medical School: 145–46
Medical services: 7, 33, 40, 51, 95, 121
Messes, unit: 64
Metric system, problem of: 38
Michigan State University: 4
Microwave systems, training in: 111
Middle Management Training Program: 110–11
Midway conference: 89–90
Mike Force (mobile strike force): 54
Military Academy: 14, 79–83, 127, 132–35. *See also* Junior Military Academy.
Military Assistance Program: 1–2, 8, 15, 18–20, 22–23, 26–29, 33, 42, 53, 55–56, 70–71, 84, 128
Military Assistance Service Funded Military Construction Program: 106–08
Military Intelligence School: 146
Military justice system: 61
Military Police School: 143–44
Military Technical Engineering School: 111–12
Militia units: 4, 8, 91. *See also* Civil Guard; Self-Defense Corps; Territorial forces.
Ministry of Defense (and War Veterans): 3, 8, 10–11, 19, 58–59, 93–96
Ministry of Economy: 95–96
Ministry of the Interior: 10, 18
Ministry of Veterans Affairs: 94–96
Mobile advisory and training teams: 39, 43–45, 119–22, 127
Mobilization. *See* Conscription programs; Manpower procurement, retention and use; Recruiting programs.
Montagnards: 20, 39–40, 75
Morale, state of: 31–32, 34, 47, 122, 127–28
Mortar fire support: 37
Mortar units: 35
Motor vehicles: 7, 101–02
Mountain commandos: 40–41
Mutual Defense Assistance Program: 1

Napalm, combat use: 37
National Campaign Plan: 29
National Defense College: 79, 83–84, 127, 136

National Police: 4, 74, 91–92. *See also* Constabulary force.
National Public Service Decree: 57
National Security Council, U.S.: 2, 19, 21
National Training Center: 79, 108
Nha Trang: 12, 38–39, 54
Night operations: 13, 38, 104, 120, 125
Nixon doctrine. *See* Vietnamization program.
Noncommissioned officers: 98–100, 108. *See also* Leaders, lack of and training.
Noncommissioned officers schools: 14, 79, 135–36
North Africa: 5
North Vietnam: 1, 89. *See also* Viet Cong.
North Vietnamese Army: 32, 47, 85, 87–88, 90, 122. *See also* Viet Cong.

O'Daniel, Lieutenant General John W.: 1–3. *See also* United States Military Assistance Advisory Group, Vietnam.
Officer candidate schools: 12, 14, 78–79, 104
Officers
  assignment policies: 98
  commissioning system: 78–79, 127
  grade structure and authorizations: 97–98, 100
  lack of and training. *See* Leaders, lack of and training.
Offshore school program: 15–16, 43–44, 79–80, 83, 113–14, 127
Okinawa: 38–39
On-the-job training: 13, 114–16
Ordnance School: 145
Ordnance units: 7, 103
Organization and force structure, ARVN: 4, 8–12, 17–19, 29–31, 65–75, 86–91, 127

Pacification program: 21, 46–47, 53, 63, 73, 86, 90, 117, 128
Paramilitary forces: 40, 47, 49, 91, 117
Pathfinder teams: 54
Patrol tactics: 104, 120
Pay and allowances: 60–61, 63–64, 74, 93–94
Peace negotiations: 87, 89
Peers, Lieutenant General William R.: 118
Pentalateral Agreement: 1

Personnel management and services: 60, 63, 76, 78, 97–100
Personnel Systems Evaluation Committee (joint): 98
Personnel turnover: 30
Phnom Penh: 119
Photography, aerial: 24
Pilots, training program: 104, 112–14
Plans, enemy: 47, 85
Plei Do Lim: 74
Plei Me: 55
Pleiku: 9, 48
Pleiku Province: 74
Poland: 1
Political crises: 30–32, 47, 127
Political Warfare College: 138
Popular Forces: 33, 42–43, 57, 60, 65–69, 71–75, 86–88, 90–93, 96, 104, 106–08, 117, 119–22, 151
Population, control of. See Civilians, control of and support by.
Post exchange system: 63–64
Presidential Action Program, U.S.: 22–23
Program Review and Analysis Improvement Systems Evaluation: 110
Programs Evaluation Office, Laos: 4
Progress Together Program: 119
Project 640: 52
Promotion policies: 60–61, 76–77, 97–100
Propaganda. See Psychological operations.
Psychological operations: 33, 45, 51, 53, 66
Psychological operations, enemy: 49
Psychological Warfare School: 45
Psychological Warfare Subcommittee, U.S.: 45
Public works, training in: 111–12

Quang Trung Training Center: 14, 34, 105
Quartermaster units: 7
Qui Nhon: 48

Radar systems: 112
Radio equipment: 36, 111
Radiological operations. See Chemical-biological-radiological operations.
Ralliers. See Repatriation program.
Ramsey, Major General Lloyd B.: 118
Ranger training centers: 33–34, 38–39
Ranger units: 17–18, 20, 25, 33–35, 39, 54–55, 60, 68, 70–71, 91, 104, 106, 117

Rations: 63–64
Reaction forces: 67
Recoilless rifles: 102
Reconnaissance, aerial: 24
Reconnaissance missions and units: 20, 54, 67–68, 91, 94
Records, deficiencies in: 125
Recruiting programs: 12, 46–47, 55, 58–59, 61, 67, 69–70, 72, 74, 83, 85–86, 90, 104. See also Conscription programs; Manpower procurement, retention and use.
Refresher training: 126
Regional Forces: 33, 42–43, 57, 64–69, 71–75, 79, 86–93, 96, 99–100, 104, 106, 119–22, 151
Religious groups: 4, 6, 20
Repair parts. See Maintenance and repair.
Repatriation program: 55
Replacement system: 35, 66
Republic of Korea forces: 101
Republic of Vietnam Air Force: 8–9, 11, 29, 54, 67, 69, 87–89, 91, 98–100, 103, 112–14, 151
Republic of Vietnam armed forces: 2–3, 9, 151
Republic of Vietnam Army (ARVN): 29–30, 151. See also Troop units.
  Airborne Division: 110
  1st Division: 118
  2d Division: 118
  5th Division: 61–62, 119
  9th Division: 34
  22d Division: 118
  23d Division: 118
  25th Division: 34, 62
  5th Armored Cavalry Regiment: 70–71
  81st Ranger Group: 94
  22d and 23d Ranger Battalions: 70–71
  60th Signal Depot: 112
Republic of Vietnam Marine Corps: 8–9, 17, 67, 69, 87–88, 91–92, 100–101, 151
Republic of Vietnam Navy: 8–9, 11, 17, 29, 67, 69–70, 87–89, 89, 91, 98–100, 103, 151
Research and development center, U.S.: 28
Reservists, recall of: 69, 86, 97
Revolutionary Development: 53, 71
Rifles
  AK47: 47, 101
  M16: 101, 125

INDEX

Road construction and repair: 13, 111
Rome Plow: 103
Rotation program: 46, 76, 98, 126
Rusk, Dean: 22

Saigon: 9–11, 14, 25, 32, 39, 47, 49–50, 58, 60, 66, 117
School enrollments: 150
School system: 13–14, 76, 79–84, 94, 103–09, 123, 125–27, 131
Schools, U.S., training at: 15–16, 43–44, 79–80, 83, 113–14, 127
Scout units: 68, 94
Search-and-destroy operations: 20, 53
Secretary of Defense. See McNamara, Robert S.
Secretary of State. See Dulles, John Foster; Rusk, Dean.
Secretary of State for National Defense: 8, 10
Sector and subsector advisers: 50–51
Security measures and units: 4, 8, 10, 13, 18–20, 24, 32–33, 43–44, 49–50, 53–55, 67, 71, 74, 90, 96, 117, 119, 125, 127–28
Selective Service System, U.S.: 57
Self-Defense Corps: 8–10, 13, 18, 22, 24–26, 29–30, 40–43, 45, 86, 91
Senate, U.S.: 30
Signal Brigade, 1st: 112
Signal School: 111–12, 142
Signal units: 7, 26, 103, 111–12. *See also* Communications equipment and units.
Small arms program: 101–03
Small Unit Leaders Guide: 77–78
Social welfare programs: 40, 63–65
Song Mao: 38–39
Spare parts. *See* Maintenance and repair.
Special Forces units: 17, 20, 22, 29, 38–39, 54, 74, 100
Special Forces units, U.S.: 17, 20, 22, 33, 38–41, 50–51, 53–55, 74, 127
  1st Group: 12, 39
  5th Group: 32, 39, 54
  7th Group: 39
  14th Detachment: 38
Specialists, training: 4, 12, 25–26, 108, 111–16
Staffs and staff officers: 76, 98, 125
State, Department of, U.S.: 7, 20–21. *See also* Dulles, John Foster; Rusk, Dean.

Stilwell, Lieutenant General Richard G.: 118
Strategic air support: 89
Strategic Hamlet Program: 29, 45–46
Strength, ARVN, periodic: 5–6, 8–9, 18, 23, 29–31, 41, 47, 65–70, 88–91, 123, 151
Strike forces: 40–41, 54, 67
Supply operations and units: 7, 110–11, 122
Switchback Operation: 40, 115

Tactical air support: 21, 24, 36–38, 54, 109
Tactics, ARVN: 23
Tank, M48: 103
Tank units. *See* Armor units.
Task Force Saigon, U.S.: 21–22
Task Force Vietnam, U.S.: 21
Tay Ninh Province: 17
Taylor, General Maxwell D.: 23, 58–60. *See also* United States Embassy.
Technical training: 111–12, 127
Technicians. *See* Specialists, training.
Telephone communication: 111–12
Teletypewriter repair: 112
Temporary Equipment Recovery Mission: 7–8
Territorial forces: 20, 23, 31, 41–43, 54, 71–75, 85, 90, 101, 117, 119–22, 151. *See also* Civil Guard; Popular Forces; Regional Forces; Self-Defense Corps.
Territorial tactical organization: 20, 22
Terrorism: 17
Tet offensive: 85–86, 91–92, 117, 128
Thieu, Nguyen Van: 55, 93
Thu Duc Military Schools Center: 14
Tools. *See* Maintenance and repair.
Trailers. *See* Motor vehicles.
Trailwatchers: 40
Training centers: 25, 33–34, 38–39, 42–43, 46, 62, 79, 84, 104–09, 123–27
Training Command: 43
Training literature: 77–78, 124–25
Training programs: 12–16, 18–19, 22–25, 33–46, 49–51, 55–56, 63, 69, 75–80, 87, 103–30. *See also* School system.
Transportation School: 111, 144–45
Transportation services and vehicles: 7, 101–02, 110–11
Treaties. *See* Agreements, international.

Troop units. *See also* Republic of Vietnam Army.
  combat effectiveness and readiness: 17, 29–33, 35–36, 46–47, 53, 62–63, 67, 84, 88, 90, 121–22, 124, 126, 128
  command and control: 9–12, 18–22, 31–32, 41–42, 66, 72–73, 117–18
Troop units—Continued
  divisions, number, roles and training: 4, 9, 13
  expansion program: 19–20, 22–23, 25–26, 29, 33–34, 65–71, 84, 88–91, 129
  leadership in. *See* Leaders, lack of and training.
  organization and force structure: 4, 8–12, 17–19, 29–31, 65–75, 86–91, 127
  personnel turnover: 30
  replacement and rotation system: 35, 46, 66, 76, 98, 126
  strength, periodic: 5–6, 8–9, 18, 23, 29–31, 41, 47, 65–70, 88–91, 123, 151
  territorial. *See* Territorial forces.
  unproductive use: 68, 70–71
Troop units, U.S.
  combat commitment: 25, 48–53, 127–28
  deployment, buildup and withdrawals: 23–27, 29–30, 32, 39, 50–51, 86, 90, 102, 109, 112, 119, 121
  strength, periodic: 30–32, 39, 48, 86
Trucks. *See* Motor vehicles.
Truman, Harry S.: 1
Troung, Major General Ngo Quang: 118

Underwater demolition teams: 70
United States Agency for International Development: 4, 59–60, 83, 93, 95
United States Air Force: 37, 113
United States Army, Pacific: 43
United States Army, Vietnam: 64–65, 121–22
United States Army Special Forces (Provisional): 39, 45
United States Embassy: 5–6, 28, 57, 59–60, 63, 93. *See also* Heath, Donald R.; Taylor, General Maxwell D.
United States Forces, Vietnam: 27
United States Information Service: 28, 50
United States Joint Support Funds: 65
United States Marine Corps: 48, 117–18
  III Amphibious Force: 117–18
  1st Division: 118

United States Military Assistance Advisory Group, Indochina: 1–2
United States Military Assistance Advisory Group, Vietnam: 2–9, 11–16, 18–19, 21–28, 30–34, 39, 42–45. *See also* Harkins, General Paul D.; McGarr, Lieutenant General Lionel C.; O'Daniel, Lieutenant General John W.; Williams, Lieutenant General Samuel T.
United States Military Assistance Command, Vietnam: 27–29, 33–37, 40–41, 43, 45–46, 48–53, 55–56, 58–63, 65, 67, 69–71, 73, 76, 78, 80, 86, 88–90, 93–95, 98–99, 101–06, 110, 119. *See also* Abrams, General Creighton W.; Westmoreland, General William C.
United States Mission Personnel and Manpower Committee: 57
United States Naval Postgraduate School: 82
United States Navy: 24, 39, 70
United States Operations Mission: 4, 18, 28, 45, 50, 69
United States Pacific Command: 7, 17, 26–28, 84, 102. *See also* Felt, Admiral Harry D.
Unity of command: 18

Van Kiep National Training Center: 62
Veterans, care of: 61, 94–97
Viet Cong: 6, 16–17, 27, 30, 32–33, 37, 40, 44–48, 54–55, 66, 85–86, 89. *See also* North Vietnamese Army.
Vietnamization Logistics Program: 102
Vietnamization program: 85–88, 101, 110, 114, 117, 122, 128–29
Village Defense Medical Program: 40
Vocational training: 94–95
Vung Tau: 111–12

War games: 109
War weariness: 60, 128
Water supply systems: 106–08
Waterways, control of: 24
Weapons. *See also by name*.
  improvement and modernization: 101–02
  training in: 120–21
Welfare, soldier's: 60–61, 63, 78

INDEX

Westmoreland, General William C.: 32, 48–49, 51–52, 58–63, 67–68, 70–72, 74, 82–84, 89, 94–95, 101, 105, 117, 119–20, 128. *See also* United States Military Assistance Command, Vietnam.

Wheeler, General Earle G.: 53

Williams, Lieutenant General Samuel T.: 16, 18. *See also* United States Military Assistance Advisory Group, Vietnam.

Women's Armed Forces Corps: 99

Youth programs: 50

Zais, Major General Melvin: 118

www.ingramcontent.com/pod-product-compliance
Lightning Source LLC
Chambersburg PA
CBHW070802100426
42742CB00012B/2219